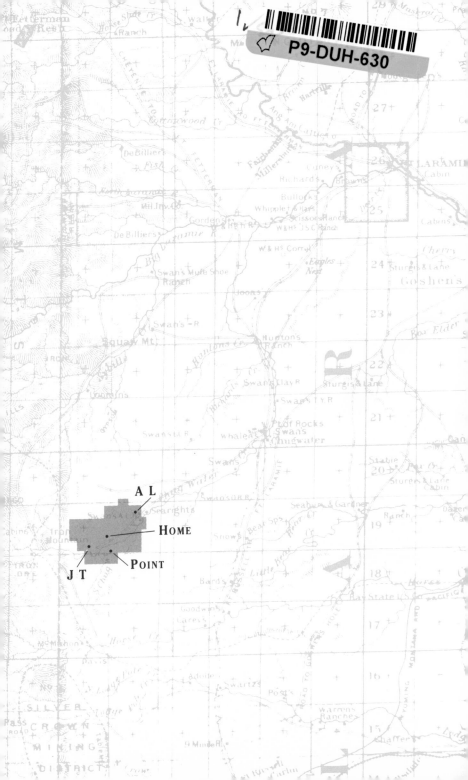

RIDING THE WHITE HORSE HOME

RIDING THE WHITE HORSE HOME

A Western Family Album

Teresa Jordan

PANTHEON BOOKS NEW YORK

All rights reserved under International and Pan-American
Copyright Conventions. Published in the United States by
Pantheon Books, a division of Random House, Inc., New York,
and simultaneously in Canada by Random House of Canada
Limited, Toronto.

"Legends" originally appeared, in slightly different form, in
Lears Magazine, March 1991, and in *The Casper Star Tribune,*
August 1 and 8, 1991.
Portions of "Walking the Hogbacks" originally appeared in the
1991 Program for the Cowboy Poetry Gathering, and in the
Spring 1992 issue of *Dry Crik Review.*

Permissions acknowledgments are on page 221.

Library of Congress Cataloging-in-Publication Data

Jordan, Teresa.
Riding the white horse home : a Wyoming family album /
Teresa Jordan.
p.   cm.
ISBN: 0-679-41219-0
1. Jordan, Teresa.   2. Ranch life—Wyoming.   3. Wyoming—
Social life and customs.   4. Wyoming—Biography.   I. Title.
CT275.J835A3   1993
978.7'19—dc20
[B]   92-26964

Book Design by M. Kristen Bearse

Manufactured in the United States of America
First Edition
2   4   6   8   9   7   5   3   1

For my family by blood
The Jordans, Steeles, and Lannens

And my family by landscape
The People of Iron Mountain

On the prairies there appeared the Phantom Horse of the West, the Ghostly Horse of the Plains, the Vision Horse of the Lakota Nation, the Rainbow Horse of the Navajo, the Iron Horse of the railroad companies, the Great White Horse Silver of the Lone Ranger, the White Steed of the Prairie.

In one thousand places and in one thousand guises the White Steed has been seen. He has been reported on the Brazos River in Texas and in the High Sierras of California. For nearly a century he has ranged over the prairies and the mountains of the West as an apparition. Hundreds of stories about him have appeared in magazines and books. But no one has ever captured him. No one ever will. It is no more possible to capture him than it is for us to recapture our lost innocence.

—Stan Steiner

CONTENTS

ACKNOWLEDGMENTS

I want first to thank my father and my brother, L.W. and Blade Jordan. They are intensely private men, and I am grateful for their help in telling this story, which is as much theirs as mine.

This book is primarily about my family in Wyoming, which is to say my father's side. My mother's family, though little mentioned in these pages, had much to do with their creation through the inspiration of their own examples—as travelers, scholars, artists, and writers. I am grateful to John and Olga Steele, Joe Steele, Dr. Frances Steele Hardin, Bob Hardin, Clarabelle Steele Parish, and Donna Parish Vowles, as well as their spouses and children.

My larger family is the Iron Mountain community itself, most especially the Farthings, Hirsigs, Bonhams, Vineyards, and Chesers. Our lives have been entwined for several generations. I wish to thank, too, those whose history in Iron Mountain is more recent, including the Dunmires, Lorenzes, and Perrys, as well as those families in Cheyenne who are adopted members of the ranch community, especially the Flynns and Crewses.

Andrea Carlisle, Patty Limerick, Joyce Thompson, and Terry Tempest Williams gave me careful readings of the manuscript, often on very short notice. I don't know what I would have done without them. Joyce Thompson also gave me, on several occasions, the lovely retreat of her family's cabin on Bainbridge Island, Washington. David Love gave me the benefit of his extraordinary knowledge of geology and the delight of his company as we rode over the Iron Mountain country on two separate occasions. Other friends and advisors have helped in more ways than I can enumerate: Martha Banyas, Christine Bourdette and Ricardo Lovett, Mary Anne Cassin, Natalie Clausen, Ardys Dance, Allen Whitaker-Emrich, John Forsgren, Linda Ganzini and Ron Heinz, Lynda Gilman, John and Donna Gray, Gene Gressley, Kristi Hager, Jim Heynen, Phil Keisling and Pam Wiley, Larry Kirkland, Bill Kittredge and Annick Smith, Bill Lazar, Diane McDevitt, David Millstone, Liz Montague, Joanne Mulcahy, Ronna Neuenschwander and Wagué Diakité, Terry O'Donnell, Doc Palen, Johanna Reilley, Bill Root and Pam Uschuck, Ron Schacter, Michael Sears, Loree Scheckels, Lillian Schlissel, Kim Stafford, Roger Stenseth, Richard Wheeler, and the staffs at the University of Wyoming Library and the Wyoming State Archives.

My editor, Dan Frank, and my agent, Kathy Robbins, alchemists both, guided this book through its many forms. I thank them for their patience, their wisdom, and their craft.

Howard Lamar first turned my head back toward my own part of the country. Richard Hart, Alvin Josephy, and the Institute of the American West gave me and many,

many others a forum and community from which to look at it afresh. The Oregon Institute of Literary Arts and the University of Montana Graduate School provided grants and precious boosts to morale. The Northwest Writing Institute, Oregon Writers' Workshop, Oregon School of Arts and Crafts, Cowboy Poetry Gathering, Haystack Program in the Arts, and Fishtrap Gathering provided invaluable employment as well as communities rich in excitement and ideas.

Finally, I want to thank my husband, Hal Cannon, and his daughter, Anneliese, for the largeness of their spirits and their love.

Riding the White Horse Home

My Family Tree

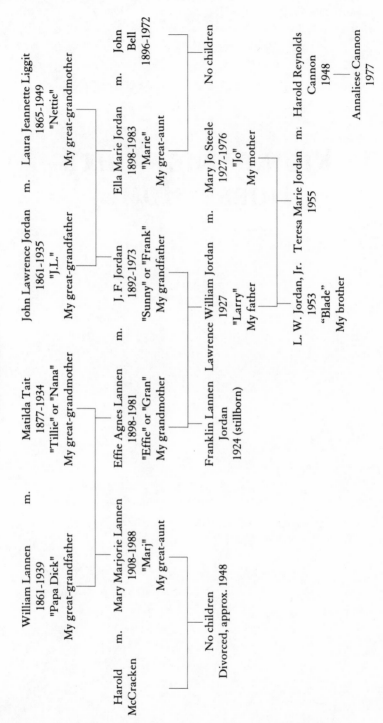

Walking the Hogbacks

A Prologue

Moving cattle along the edge of the breaks

As a young child, I used to walk the blue hogback ridges near my family's ranch in the Iron Mountain country of southeastern Wyoming with my great-grandmother, looking for fossils and arrowheads. Nana—Matilda Tait Lannen, my father's mother's mother—lived in town, but she loved to come to the ranch. Though well over eighty, she was tireless as she hiked the steep hills in her flowered dress, her sturdy walking shoes, and a battered, flat-brimmed straw hat. Walking with her was magic, for she could find crinoids or Indian relics almost anywhere we stepped. It was a matter of looking, she said, of learning to see.

Nana died when I was eight years old, and a couple of

years later the family gave me her silver-inlaid spurs. They became my proudest possession and I used them daily in the horse and cow work that made up my childhood. Oddly, I didn't connect these spurs with Nana until much later. I knew they had been hers, but I guess I thought of them as something she collected, like the petrified wood and colorful agates that crowded the shelves in her apartment. She had ranched with her husband, but they sold their ranch and moved to town in 1914, some forty years before I was born. The Nana I knew played bridge at the Country Club and smelled of lilac and cedar. I couldn't imagine her on a horse.

Twenty years after Nana died, my great-aunt on the other side of my father's family, Marie Jordan Bell, told me that she used to visit the Lannens and sit on the fence while Nana sorted horses. "Her husband would say, 'Tillie, you do the cutting,' and she'd do the whole thing. She was perfect with a blacksnake, just perfect. One crack of the whip and those horses would go just where she wanted them."

My great-grandmother, high-booted, wearing silver-mounted spurs, standing in a corral surrounded by galloping horses, directing them this way and that with a bullwhip —how had I missed this side of her? If she were alive, she might have told me that I needed only to look.

The ranch where I was raised is located fifty miles northwest of Cheyenne, fifty miles northeast of Laramie, and twenty-six miles southwest of Chugwater. The best road goes to Cheyenne and we did our business there; when people in Iron Mountain refer to "town," they generally mean Cheyenne.

The ranch stretches along eight miles of Chugwater Creek in what is the narrowest part of the Chugwater Valley. My family lived there for four generations, from the time my great-grandfather first arrived from Maryland in 1887 until 1978, the year after I graduated from college. The Jordans are considered a pioneer family in Wyoming, but our history is short compared to that of the native tribes that once moved across this land and only a footnote to the great reaches of time that shaped the land itself.

The hogbacks that I used to explore with Nana form the northwest edge of the valley, anywhere from two to five miles away from the creek, and a line of breaks, about a mile on the other side of the stream, forms the other. These hogbacks once lay flat, the floor of a series of seas that advanced and retreated several times across this part of North America. The fossilized crinoids, snails, and clams that Nana and I collected once lived in those seas. After the water withdrew for the last time, around sixty-five million years ago, sections of the sea floor rose up on end in what geologists call the Laramide Revolution and formed the part of the Rocky Mountains known as the Laramie Range. Hogback ridges, composed primarily of limestone, extend east off that range and are shaped like big hams. Some are rounded, like uncut hams, and some have flat faces, like hams that have been sliced. The two rows of hogbacks that run through our ranch are "sliced," rising in arcs and then disappearing back into the ground rather like the scales of a stegosaurus. They are between a 150 million and 250 million years old. Behind them, the larger, rounded hogbacks are even older.

The breaks that form the other side of the Chugwater Valley are "sweet young things," having risen over a mile from sea level with the rest of the Great Plains only twenty or thirty million years ago. They are the sort of breaks that form the background for almost every Western movie, many-fingered land forms that rise at steep angles, striated in various shades of gray and white and pink, dotted with sagebrush and mountain mahogany. On top of them is rolling grassland that stretches as far as the eye can see and makes good summer pasture.

The valley itself consists primarily of green meadowland. Our ranch was known as a good hay ranch and we never kept more cattle than our own meadows could support. In a drought year, we sold down the herd. The willows and box elders that line the creek provide shelter: during the '49 blizzard, a historic storm that wiped out whole herds, we lost only eight head of cattle.

At an altitude of over six thousand feet, Iron Mountain is great country for wind. In the winter, it blows for weeks on end with hardly a dip below twenty or thirty miles an hour. Gusts of fifty and sixty miles an hour are common. Snow doesn't melt, people say, it just wears out. Someone who asks if the wind ever quits is likely to be told that it does, long enough to change directions. I once ran across a list of nearly four hundred winds from around the world and wondered why Wyoming, so dominated by wind, has so few names for its variations. The only one that came to mind was chinook. "I can think of a few more," our neighbor, Wayne Bonham, suggested. "There's the wind, the damned wind, and the goddamned wind."

Ranchers cuss the wind, but they have much to thank it for. The meadows that make ranching possible in this part of Wyoming blew in 15 to 20 million years ago, from volcanic eruptions in Idaho and Utah and Nevada. The wind then excavated the hogbacks and carved out the Chugwater Valley, leaving a rich clayey soil that drains well and never goes sour. Sometimes, though, on days when the gale hurtles pebbles through the air with enough force to break the skin, the meadows seem ready to move on.

There are places on the ranch where horizontal layers of the 30-million-year-old breaks butt right up against the 250-million-year-old vertical planes of the hogbacks. At this point, over 200 million years of geologic history disappear. Geologists call this missing record an unconformity. "We know where we were and we know where we are," the field geologist David Love once told me, "but it's not always clear how we got here from there."

David Love has spent his lifetime wandering around Wyoming, looking for continuity, trying to unravel the mystery. He has completed two statewide field maps and reads the landscape like a book. He has, in my great-grandmother's terms, learned how to see. Still, he says, there is much he doesn't understand. He tells me that the ranch where I was raised is rich in unconformities.

I think of an unconformity as something similar to the white space or break on the page writers sometimes use to leap from one idea to another. Or perhaps an unconformity is like all that hazy history that lies between the legends we have of our ancestors and the realities of our own particular lives.

My favorite spot on the ranch was the Point, the place on top of the breaks where I could see forever. It would take me an hour to ride up the steep ridge trail and then I would dismount, letting my horse graze while I sat cross-legged for hours, absentmindedly casting pebbles down the steep slope. Almost everything I could see I called home. The ranch headquarters, the group of buildings where my family lived, was on the far side of Chugwater Creek—the stone house my great-grandfather had built in 1890, the ice house, the cookhouse, the bunkhouse, the garage with a second bunkhouse in its attic, the shop, the coal house, the huge barn and its set of horse corrals, and, nearer the creek, the big set of cattle corrals. Our foreman lived two miles up the creek at the set of buildings we called the J T—a white house which would, a few years later, burn on Fathers' Day, an unpainted barn, a calving shed, more corrals. And five miles below our house, further down the creek at the far end of the ranch, cottonwoods hid the set of buildings where another hired man and his family lived: the A L.

Up behind our house, toward the hogbacks on Three Mile Creek, was the dazzling blue patch of the reservoir, the catch pond that provided us with irrigation water to supplement our water right on Chug. I could trace the track of that water through a system of ditches that my great-grandfather, grandfather, and father had dug to turn the good meadows green. I would not have articulated such a thought at the time, but I was looking at the history of my family, at the mark we had made on the land.

I was looking, as well, at the histories of other families, for our ranch was stitched together from dozens of homesteads and smaller ranches. The particular despair of families seduced by their government onto plots of land too small to support them is remembered now only through place names: the Fox Place, Jones Spring, the Krissel. The J T and the A L were named for the cattle brands once associated with them. The failure of the vast open-range operations figured into the quilt as well. Both our Swan Meadow and the A L had once belonged to the Swan Land and Cattle Company, the Scottish enterprise that James Michener used as a model for his novel *Centennial*.

There were reminders, too, of those who had occupied the land long before the coming of cattle—Arapahoe, Cheyenne, Lakota Sioux. Behind me in the Top Pasture were what we called tepee rings, circles of stones laid out in the prairie grass. Almost anywhere on the ranch we were likely to find arrowheads and sometimes larger implements— spear points, pounding stones, hatchet heads. Looking out from the Point, I would squint my eyes and I could see the land as I believed it had once been, unmarked by ditches or roads or power lines or the railroad, smoke rising in thin wisps from a small group of tepees. Sometimes, while I sat lost in such dreams, I would look down from the Point to see a hawk riding the updrafts from the ridges below me and I would think: I am higher than he is. This is what it's like to fly.

It was the custom of many in the country to never carry water. Drinking, we thought, just made us more thirsty. The men chewed tobacco, but my father had taught me to put a small stone in my mouth. It gave the tongue something to work on and thirst would magically disappear. I always looked for a particular type of rock, a pink quartz conglomerate, because I liked its feel, and I can still conjure its taste and its reassuring sense of moisture. I once dreamt that my teeth were made of such stones and it was a comforting dream, as if the font of everything I needed, water and land, was right inside my mouth. That's what I felt, on a larger scale, from my viewpoint at the top of the breaks: that I had some direct connection to both the land and the events that transpired upon it.

If I had only been to the Point one time, I would never forget it. Such expansiveness shapes the synapses in irreversible ways. But I did not visit the Point a single time. I went time after time and hour after hour. I thought I could always return. However vaguely I understood that every tribe and every family that had once called the Chugwater Valley home had been forced to leave, I could not imagine my own family moving on. I could not imagine that in twenty or twenty-five years I would remember the Point from another life in another state, and that in the intervening years our ranch would have passed out of my family and into another, and finally into the hands of an oil company.

. . .

My grandfather, the man we all called Sunny, died in 1973. His death signaled the start of what I now look back on as more than a decade of loss. Our family had not accomplished the estate planning that would have eased transfer of the ranch, and we could not afford to keep it. It was sold in 1978 and we moved off the land almost exactly ninety years after my great-grandfather first arrived.

There were other losses. My mother died suddenly and unexpectedly from an aneurysm during my junior year of college in 1976. Then, over the next few years, the rest of my father's small family, the side of the family I was raised with, died. By 1988 the only ones left were my father, my brother, and me. I lost, too, an uncanny number of friends to accidents and cancer.

I was raised to be Western, which is to say stoic. I think sometimes of the word "frontier," that concept that has figured so largely in American life with its promise, always, of a fresh start. "Frontier" comes from the Old English word *frowntere,* the front line of an army. And *frowntere* comes from the Old French *fronter* or *frontier,* which is the word for front brow. For years I forged ahead and never looked back. I returned to college from my mother's death and graduated on time. I wrote a book. I was offered another contract. I seemed launched on a successful career.

But under it all was an increasing sense of unease. After graduation in 1977, I worked on the ranch for a final summer and then knocked around the South and the Northeast before I moved to Casper, Wyoming. I moved to Denver. I moved to Portland, Oregon. I moved back to the Iron

Mountain country, to a neighboring ranch. I moved back to Portland. I moved to Missoula, Montana, for a year of graduate school. I moved to Butte, Montana. I was unable to finish another book, unable to maintain a relationship, exhausted all the time and yet filled with an anxiety that made me want to crawl out of my skin. Often I felt like I was already out of my skin, perched high up in some corner of the room watching a stranger down below who looked like me but did the oddest things.

In 1987, I moved to Portland for the third time and bought a 1920s bungalow in poor repair. Once again, the move brought no relief. An on-and-off relationship that had dragged on for seven years came to a sudden end; the house, in much worse shape than I had realized, seemed to be falling down around my ears; my work was a mess but I had no idea what else I might do.

I have always tried to escape anxiety with busyness and I dove into work on the house, first building bookcases for my study. When they were done and I started to fill them, I dropped a book and it fell open on the floor in front of me. It was *The Human Community* by Baker Brownell and a line leapt out at me: "Our little century of escape is about over."

I had come across the book in Montana when I was doing research for a community study. The sentence must have struck me at the time, for I had underlined it. Now, lying open on the floor, it seemed almost to glow. I remembered thinking, I wish my little decade of escape would end. In retrospect, that moment stands as the point when I finally quit pushing blindly ahead and began to turn around and take stock of where I'd been. It was then, I suppose, that I first started trying to excavate the unconformities that connect my heritage with who I am now, that I began to learn how to see.

When I turned around I had to confront not only the loss of people I loved and land that had defined my family for nearly a century but also a way of life. My family was not alone when we left ranching. We were part of an exodus of over 14 million people who have left the land during my lifetime.

The Iron Mountain I knew as a child was a community in which families had worked side by side for three and four generations. Today, only one ranch is run by the same family it was fifteen years ago. The couple of hundred square miles that comprise the neighborhood supported two or three hundred people in my grandfather's day, perhaps a hundred and fifty when my father was a child, sixty or seventy when I lived there. Today, roughly half the land area, including two long-time family ranches, belongs to the True Oil Company, and another ranch was sold to an investor, for an amount far above its agricultural value, as a retreat. The school is closed, the post office is closed, the teacherage and store and railroad station have burned down, and fewer than thirty people, counting children, live in all those miles and miles.

For thousands of years, most people lived and worked on the land. Only in the last century have we "come indoors." Today, less than 2 percent of Americans live on farms and ranches. As Lewis Hyde noted in his study of community and creativity, *The Gift,* "The spirit of a community or collective can be wiped out, tradition can be destroyed. We tend to think of genocide as the physical destruction of a race or group, but the term may be aptly expanded to include the obliteration of the *genius* of a group, the killing of its creative spirit."

When I turned around to look at Iron Mountain, I saw hundreds of examples of the particular genius required by a life tied to land and animals and seasons: the house I grew up in was built into the hill for insulation and shelter from the wind; the barn, too, was built into the hill so that hay could be unloaded directly into its loft. The design of each building, each corral, each ditch, was tied directly to the creative act of staying alive. So was the interdependence of the people who lived there, the design of the community itself. Even the name for Chugwater comes from the genius of survival. Before they acquired guns, Native Americans ran buffalo off a high cliff into the creek. When the animals hit the water, they made a chugging sound. One good run provided enough meat and hides to feed, clothe, and house the tribe for a year.

There have been no buffalo in Iron Mountain for over a century, and today there are few humans. This is a book about a place and the people attached to it, about a way of life that has almost disappeared. It came out of my attempt to understand the forces that shaped me, which are in large part the forces that shaped the rural West. Because this is a book about loss, it is much involved with the process of grieving, but it has allowed me to know where I came from. In that knowing, I have a way to keep my people with me and also let them go. I have a way to hold to the land.

A few years before my Great-aunt Marie died, I visited her at her ranch on the North Fork of Chugwater Creek and we went out early in the morning to feed the bulls. Marie was practically blind then. I drove the pickup through the center of the meadow and the bulls gathered around for their taste of hay and cottonseed cake. Marie pointed to a hill in the distance. "There's a couple up there that don't seem so interested," she said. "We better kick them down."

I looked where she pointed. "I think those are rocks, Marie."

"No," she said, "they're bulls."

Marie was blind enough that she could no longer recognize neighbors at the post office, and just that morning she had mistaken the baler for a pickup.

"I really think those are rocks, Marie."

"There's never been any rocks there before," she said.

To indulge her, I pointed the long-bed pickup up the hill. I could see that the dark spots on the hill were just rocks, but I held my tongue. Marie would see soon enough. We were still a hundred yards away when the rocks rose slowly to their feet and began to wag their great white heads as they lumbered in to feed.

My Great-aunt Marie and my great-grandmother were women who had learned to see. Marie could read the landscape even through her shattered sky-blue eyes and Nana could pluck fossils and arrowheads off barren ground like a magician might pull pigeons from his sleeve. These women make me train my own eye. These women make me write.

Legends

My great-grandfather J. L. Jordan

My grandfather disliked children and cats. He was a grand old ranchman who pulled his boots on first and his britches on after, who never went outside without a hat. He chain-smoked Camels, pinched between thumb and middle finger or dangling from the corner of his mouth. Sunny—even my brother and I called him by his nickname —would never have held a smoke "like a goddamned dilettante," between two outstretched fingers, and he flicked the butts a good ten yards after stubbing them out. He dressed meticulously, in starched khaki shirts and five-button Levi's, pressed to a knife-edge crease.

Sunny was crippled up from too many bad horses and too much bad weather. I don't remember ever seeing him ride; I only remember him angry that he couldn't. He some-times stomped from the house and roared away in his Cad-illac to find the hired men and cause some sort of trouble for my dad, but mostly he stayed home and surveyed the ranch from the picture windows of his second-floor apart-ment in the Big House.

I learned to count by playing blackjack with Sunny while the big Siamese slept on his lap. In the summer, if the cat went hunting or I helped outside, my grandfather would scowl around downstairs. "Where's that damn cat?" he'd ask my mother. "Where's that kid?"

I feared my grandfather, but I also loved him. He played fair, and he played often. He wasn't much of a talker; mostly, he chewed on a toothpick and studied his cards. Still, he taught me necessary lessons. By the time I started school, I knew better than to cut a blackjack deck, touch my cards before the deal was done, or expose my own good fortune with a smile. Occasionally, he would remi-nisce, like the time the song "House of the Rising Sun" came on the old Philco. "I was there once," he said of the Louisiana whorehouse as he gazed out the window. And then, as if he remembered he was with me and not my brother, he flicked his cards abruptly. "Hit me," he said. I dealt him a queen. He tossed his toothpick in my pile.

Sunny received his nickname, I've been told, from his sunny disposition. By the time I knew him, he was mostly humorless, often angry. I realize now he was also tender, but tenderness embarrassed him and he disguised it with gruffness. Finally, he grew bitter, and then he grew old.

When I was seven, Sunny had a minor stroke. Soon after, he bought a ranch in Montana. The purchase was a bad decision, but he realized he was coming to the end of his life, and he had not accomplished what he set out to do —he was not the biggest rancher in Wyoming, not in Laramie County, not even on Chugwater Creek. The Montana ranch was a last attempt.

Though he borrowed enough money to gain control of some fifty sections outside Miles City—a ranch nearly as large as the one we already ran at Iron Mountain—the venture overextended us. Drought and several calving seasons where the mercury never climbed higher than twenty below left us a hairsbreadth from disaster. We nearly lost both ranches. When Sunny asked my father to cosign yet another note, my father refused unless he also took control. Sunny had no choice; he handed over the reins. We sold the Montana place and hunkered down at home to fend off the bankers. Night after night, I remember waking to hear my father pace in the hall.

In his decline, Sunny bought a stud—a range thoroughbred, seventeen hands tall, high-withered, Roman-nosed, so mean no one could ride him. The stud ran free on the ranch with a dozen mares, all also unbroken.

We wrangled the stud bunch every spring, and Sunny would watch from his bedroom window as we ran them into the corral. We would rope off the yearlings to wean and the three-year-olds to break. Before I was old enough to join in the horse breaking, I would stand at the window by my grandfather, listening to him suck down his Camels until they almost singed his fingers, hearing him chuckle as the colts stomped my father or one of the men into the ground.

The stud's blood made the colts mean. Light-footed in the front, they struck to kill. In a decade, we managed to break only four out of fifty or more. The rest ended up at rodeos, and when they proved too mean to handle there, they ended up as soap.

My grandfather loved that stud, loved the mares, loved the colts no one could break. He loved the thought that he had ridden, when he was young, tougher colts than the stud could ever throw. Through the years, as I watched him watch the colts, he grew older. Bald as a baby, bent-backed, he sometimes dribbled on the khaki shirts he had prided himself all his life on keeping clean.

Sunny died when I was eighteen, and I came home from my freshman year of college for the funeral. At the grave site, I broke down. Though my tears surprised that gathering of Westerners bred never to reveal emotion, they surprised no one more than me. I had not realized before how much I cared for Sunny, how much that man who disliked cats and children cared for me.

During all the time I spent with Sunny, he told me few family stories. About the founder of the Jordan Ranch, Sunny's father and my Great-grandfather J.L., he told me only one, but he told it often. It was the Family Legend, the story of J.L.'s coming to Wyoming, a story as important to my

grandfather as a creation myth is to a Mandan Indian. It
went like this.

J.L. grew up in Maryland. When the Civil War broke
out, he wanted to join his brothers who had already gone to
fight. But J.L. was just fourteen and his parents said no. He
did the only thing a self-respecting fourteen-year-old could
do—he ran away from home. The war ended before J.L.
arrived at the front; since he couldn't go back to his family,
he started out West. He worked his way across the country,
building bridges in Illinois and railroads in Nebraska.
When he arrived in Wyoming, he went to work for a fellow
named Collins on Chugwater Creek. Collins died and J.L.
was owed a couple of years' wages; he took out a mechanic's
lien and got title to what would become the core of
the Jordan Ranch. Through the years Great-grandfather
bought more cattle and more land, and he never wrote
home until he had made himself into a success.

It's a splendid story, one which I have told through the
years with pride. The only problem is, it's not quite true.
J.L. was born in 1861. He would have been four years old
when Lee surrendered. In fact, he didn't leave home until
the fall of 1886, at the age of twenty-five, and then with the
family's blessing. He did work his way across the country,
he did take a job with Collins on Chugwater Creek, and he
did end up with title in lieu of wages. But he had not
severed ties with his paternal home, as my grandfather
would have it. Rather, J.L.'s Western adventure was tightly
interwoven with the folks back home.

"Have been looking for a letter from home all this

week," J.L. wrote his father in November 1886 from Ash-
land, Nebraska, where he worked with a bridge gang.
"Have been thinking a good bit about Home and last night
one year ago when Ma died," he wrote the following
February.

In Cheyenne, the family network helped him establish
himself. He boarded with a Presbyterian minister from Virginia who knew his family. Collins, too, was not a complete
stranger: he was the cousin of J.L.'s betrothed, Laura Jeannette Liggit. Later, J.L. borrowed money from his father to
buy a herd in partnership with Collins.

And J.L. never quit pining for home. "I am well and
enjoying myself pretty well although think could enjoy myself better in Md," he wrote in November of 1887. "But
have not forgotten the old lesson you taught me. Business
before pleasure." His letters are full of pleas for his father
to visit, and for his brothers to take up land nearby.

Even the first record I have from Sunny shows the
family tie. "Dear Grandpa," he wrote at the age of six, on
August 27, 1898, to J.L.'s father back in Maryland, "We
have 200 calves. We are breaking 2 coalts. 1 black and 1
buck-skin. I like to take care of my sister. Tell Uncle Otho
I have a good saddle. He had better come back. Good bye.
Frank Jordan."

It's not surprising that Sunny's version of the Family
Legend departs from the facts. As one historian has suggested, history is what we remember; personal history, I
suspect, is what we want to believe. What is interesting is
not that the story changed, but that it changed in such
predictable ways. Sunny turned his father into an orphan

cast into the Western wilderness alone; a prodigal who returned to his familial home only in triumph and never to stay, who raised his own fatted calf, branded it, and shipped it east in a railroad car.

A little over a year and a half before J.L. reached Iron Mountain, another young man from the East passed through. On Independence Day, 1885, twenty-five-year-old Owen Wister spent the night at a stage station on Chugwater Creek. "We're 8200 feet up in the air & it's cold," he wrote his mother. "The air is better than all other air. Each breath you take tells you no one else has ever used it before you—the scenery would not please you except now & then. It's very wild & desolate."

This was Wister's first trip West. He would one day write *The Virginian,* a novel about an orphan who left home at the age of fourteen and came to Wyoming. It would sell more copies than any other Western. For now, the young Harvard graduate was getting a taste of the west on orders from his doctor, a prescribed rest cure for "hysteria"— blinding headaches, terrifying dreams, hallucinations. When he left Wyoming at the end of his two-month trip, his health was much improved and he had fallen in love with the West. He entered Harvard Law, but probably he had already made up his mind to be a writer. In 1892, the same year that J.L's twelve-pound son was delivered kicking and screaming into the high Wyoming air, Wister published his first Western stories. Among them was "How Lin McLean Went East."

Lin McLean, a cowboy just returned from the roundup, heard a sermon on the prodigal son. For the first time in eight years, he missed his ancestral home in Massachusetts. His folks were dead, but he had a brother and he was suddenly homesick. He decided to go East, but he wasn't "going to show up plumb broke like the feller did after eatin' with the hogs." He worked until he could "buy the fatted calf [him]self, you bet!"

When he arrived in Boston, his rough Western appearance embarrassed his brother. They quarreled and Lin left. He headed back West filled with a "deep hatred of the crowded, scrambling East."

"It weren't home I had went to back East," he says as he sees the Wind River country again. "Now this country here . . . seein' it onced more, I know where my home is, and I wouldn't live nowheres else. Only I ain't got no father watching for me to come up Wind River." Lin McLean, the disappointed prodigal, the orphan, would stay West to make his own life, alone.

"Lin McLean's failure to find a father in either East or West thus became the cowboy's peculiar virtue," wrote Wister's chronicler, Ben Merchant Vorpahl. "To be American he had to remain alien, even in America."

Sunny may have felt the need to orphan his father because he felt like an orphan himself. Shortly after my father was born, Sunny and J.L. quarreled—over what, no one remembers—and Sunny moved to town. He worked as an insurance agent and later as assistant insurance commissioner. He would hardly have made a happy salesman under the best of conditions; then, during the Great Depression, he was surely miserable. My father remembers sitting at the kitchen table while Sunny glued soles on his oxfords. My grandfather was a physically powerful man but not a dexterous one; the task itself infuriated him almost as much as being reduced to doing it in the first place. I can imagine him hunched over the shoe, his cigarette quivering as he swore through clenched teeth, ashes falling into the glue.

J.L. died in 1935. Sunny returned to the ranch. Over the argument no one now remembers, they had never made peace.

Sunny was lucky to have a ranch to go back to. Almost from the time J.L. had arrived in Iron Mountain forty years earlier, he had thought of leaving. On May 29, 1887, he wrote his father in Maryland, "[I] dont lik the country well enough to stay in it long . . . think if I stay till fall that will wind up Wyoming for me." By fall, however, he had decided to buy cattle, though the critters didn't fill his loneliness. "This is Sunday," he wrote some months later, "and it's the most lonesome I ever saw. They can say what they please about a Far West Life but it takes a good bit of sand to stick to it espetialy me in the cow business." In 1890 he returned to Maryland, married Laura Jeannette, and brought her back to Iron Mountain.

By the next year, they had decided to sell the Wyoming ranch and buy one in Nebraska near members of Nettie's family. "Am shure can make more money out here [than in

Nebraska]," J.L. wrote his father on August 16, 1891. "But Nettie doesant have much company out here and that is the reason would like to own the [Nebraska] place. . . ."

After they had arranged the sale, J.L. wrote, "Well I never hated to leave a country as bad as do this one. It just spoils me but don't think it is the country to keep a woman in." Somehow, J.L. had forgotten his own complaints about the weather and the isolation; the move would be "for Nettie's sake."

For a reason never made clear in the letters, the deal fell through. In a few more years, the couple considered selling out again, and this time J.L. was more willing to acknowledge his part. "I am involved a good deal with rheumatism," he complained in a letter dated April 19, 1898. "Think sometimes I will sell out but have not fully decided." By June, he was more resolute: "I think we will sell out this fall if we can to advantage. Want $30,000. There is few young men that has a better thing than I have but Nettie does not have good health here and I am not so ruggid as I once was. . . . I have seen very few of this world's plasures and have known nothing but work and I think if I am ever going to make a change I had better do it soon."

Once again, for reasons that aren't clear, they kept the ranch. Years later, Sunny would remember vague talk about selling, but he would attribute it solely to his mother's unhappiness. So did his sister, my Great-aunt Marie. "Mother was a great woman, really," she told me once. "But she didn't like living on the ranch. Every year she'd say, 'Now this will be our last year, won't it?' And Dad would say, 'Yes.' He had no more idea of moving off of there than I had."

Owen Wister described his character Lin McLean as "not only a good man, but a man. This somehow counts for more in Wyoming." McLean earned this praise because he was physically strong, competent to meet the challenges of an undeveloped land, and had both integrity and a good sense of humor. A miner in Butte, Montana, once described another worker similarly: "He was a big man, more powerful than he himself really knew. He could *do* things."

Not only a good man, but a man. He could *do* things. These simple words capture much of what I respect most about my great-grandfather, my grandfather, my father, and the other men who surrounded my upbringing. They could *do* things. Any one of them could feed four hundred cattle, day after day, alone in a Wyoming winter, build a house from stone they had quarried themselves, or line out a dozen miles of irrigation ditch at a 1 percent grade with only a thirty-six-inch measure and a hundred-yard length of chain.

But if these ranchers could work alone, they also worked together. Each spring kicked off an unofficial race among the families in Iron Mountain to repair shared fence lines. Necessary labors such as brandings, roundups, and trail drives were neighborhood festivities. Smoke from a grass fire would cause every single hand on every single ranch to drop whatever he or she was doing and respond.

The history of the West is the story of cooperation, not isolation. As the Western historian Bernard De Voto has quipped, the only true rugged individualists were usually found dangling from a rope held by a group of cooperating citizens.

As important to my grandfather as his reputation as a good cattleman was his name as a good neighbor. Still, he was shaped by a primitivist urge, by a belief that his father had done it all alone and so should he. He was quick to offer help, uneasy when he needed it in return. By some twist of logic, community was commendable, but should flow only one way. In Sunny's notion of who he should be, there was little room for loneliness, for doubt, for mutual dependence. "I kill my own snakes," Sunny was wont to say, "and bury my own dead."

There are a few rules to ranching that mustn't be broken. One is that you rise at five-thirty each morning. In the winter, this means that you sit at the kitchen table and drink coffee for hours before it's light enough to work, but you get up early because a neighbor might drive by and know you were still abed.

A second rule is that ranchers don't take vacations. In good years, if Dad could get away, we would spend a weekend in the Brown Palace Hotel in Denver. We would visit the zoo and the natural history museum, see our annual movie, go out to dinner. These weekends were enchanted. But a real vacation, where we might be gone for several days or even two weeks—that was unthinkable.

When I was eight years old, my mother, my brother, and I went to Yellowstone Park with my godmother and her two kids. It never occurred to me that my father might have come along; it didn't seem strange that we had left him at the ranch even though he was laid up with a broken leg, in plaster from toe to hip. The trip to Yellowstone was a lark, a high point of my childhood. I was completely unaware of its undercurrents, or the fact that it had almost torn our family asunder.

A few weeks before, a horse had fallen on my father and crushed his leg. Soon after he got home from the hospital, he realized there was little he could do around the ranch when he couldn't walk, ride, or drive. "Jo and I have been wanting to take the kids to Yellowstone," he told Nelson Vineyard, our foreman. "I think I'll get out of your hair." My father wanted to put Nelson's name on the ranch checking account so he could cover emergencies if Sunny were unavailable. Then Dad went to Sunny with his plan. Sunny's response was immediate. "You aren't good for anything else; the least you can do is stick around and sign the goddamned checks."

I was thirty-three years old when Nelson told me this story; I had never had a clue of it before. When I asked my father about it, he grew quiet. "Yes," he said, "I remember it. I was so angry that day I would have walked off the ranch and never looked back. But I had no money of my own then. Nothing, not a cent. Laid up like I was, I had no chance of getting another job for at least six months. I had a wife and two children. I backed down."

My father is proud of his life. He served in Germany

and in Korea. He took a bankrupt ranch and made it financially sound. He once crawled down a canyon two miles with a broken leg. Only in this encounter with his father did he question his courage. "Ye need be a coward but once," he said.

"Dad," I said, "when somebody is sick or hurt, it's natural for people around them to be angry for a while. Wouldn't Sunny have come to his senses in a day or two?"

"Sunny wasn't like that," Dad replied.

I have a rancher friend, a man, who suggests that the West can be understood as the history of fathers fighting sons. Of the four ranches in the greater Iron Mountain area that have passed from father to son in my lifetime, only one made the transition with grace. One father died without a will; two others, including my grandfather, had not done the estate planning that would have made transition easy, even possible. I have found, after driving sixty thousand miles of ranch country back roads from Montana to Texas and Oklahoma to California, that Iron Mountain is hardly unique.

The usual explanation for these men who failed to prepare for their deaths is that they thought they would never die. But ranchers are nothing if not realists, living day in and day out with the possibility of death. I believe the explanation stems from a much deeper, unconscious reluctance, and I believe it comes directly from the primitivist urge that glorifies man alone and makes him believe he should be able to succeed entirely by himself. If a man can't live up to who he thinks *he* should be, how can his son ever live up to him?

When my brother Blade was born, my grandfather opened a charge account for him at the Brown Palace Bar. When I was born a year and a half later, Sunny made a gesture of comparable generosity, but no one remembers exactly what it was. Probably, he purchased life insurance or contributed to my savings account; whatever the gift, it held few of the expectations for me that a credit line at one of the West's most famous saloons held for my brother.

From the start, Sunny and Blade were like oil and water. Blade didn't stand straight enough for my grandfather; he didn't speak loudly enough or sit a horse right. He worked on the ranch and made a good hand—he could ride, rope, doctor cattle, fix fence—but these were not skills he particularly enjoyed or at which he chose to excel. A happy-go-lucky kid who liked to read and draw and play superheroes in the hayloft, he had no taste for killer broncs. My brother would not have run away from home at the age of fourteen to go to war.

It was easier for me to please Sunny and my dad. With no expectation that I would work outside at all, they took the fact that I liked their world as not only a surprise but a compliment. Dad had more patience with me than he did with my brother, and he liked to teach me things—how to shift my weight when training a horse to rein, how to double-clutch the stock truck, how to hog-tie a calf. Along with these physical skills, I learned early what most women raised on ranches know: that it's easier to be a rancher's daughter than a rancher's son. Pushed off into the eddies of family history, we don't have to strong-arm the rapids.

My brother left the ranch as soon as he was able. He became an oil-field roughneck, joined the paratroopers, went to gunsmithing school, and now works as a Harley-Davidson mechanic. He seldom calls home.

The first thing my father did after Sunny's funeral was sell the mare and stud bunch. Next, he listed the ranch for sale. Blade didn't want the ranch; I did, but I doubt, even if I were male, I could have had it. Ranching wasn't fun for my father anymore, and he wanted out. A lifetime of injuries had left him with a pinched nerve in his neck, a slipped disc in his back, and arthritis all over. Estate taxes were devastating—annual interest on the loan required to pay them exceeded the profit the ranch generated even during its best years. We might have sold part of it in order to keep the rest, but my father chose not to. Dividing the ranch would limit its income as well; if I came back as an adult to participate in management, the resources would be spread thinner yet. Besides, Dad had brought the ranch back from the brink once and he was unwilling to do it again. If he were trying to explain his reasons, he might have hearkened back to J.L.: "I have seen very few of this world's plasures and have known nothing but work and I think if I am ever going to make a change I had better do it soon."

Because it was something she could not imagine her own father doing, my Great-aunt Marie never forgave my father for selling the ranch; because the ranch was something I so much wanted for my: If, forgiveness came hard for me, too.

Alexis de Tocqueville, the young Frenchman who visited America in 1831, saw a danger in this country where "new families are constantly springing up, others are constantly falling away, and all that remain change their condition. . . . [Americans]," he said, "owe nothing to any man, they expect nothing from any man; they acquire the habit of always considering themselves as standing alone, and they are apt to imagine that their whole destiny is in their own hands. Not only does democracy make every man forget his ancestors, but it hides his descendants and separates his contemporaries from him; it throws him back forever upon himself alone, and threatens in the end to confine him entirely within the solitude of his own heart."

When we see ourselves or our kin measuring up short of the legends that shape us, our disappointments turn into blame—of a government that interferes, of a wife who would make us move, of a son who isn't "ruggid" enough, of a father who chooses not to ranch forever. Unable to accept our own shortcomings or forgive those of our kin, we orphan ourselves within the solitude of our own hearts.

When Blade was eight and I was six, we decided to run away from home. We announced our intentions to our mother, and she made us peanut butter sandwiches and poured us thermoses of milk. She helped us tie these provisions, with some fruit and candy bars, into hobo handkerchiefs that we hung on sticks and slung over our shoulders. Our ultimate destination was Chugwater, twenty-six miles away, but we hoped to make it five miles to the Vineyards, who lived at the far end of the ranch, by nightfall.

By noon we had walked about three miles and were almost to the railroad trestle over Chugwater Creek. We were preparing to scramble down the bank and have lunch when we saw a rider galloping toward us. It was Dad. Of course, we stopped and waited.

A horse running across a pasture in the heat of the summer really does kick up a trail of dust, and it's something grand to see. Our father sat a fine figure on a horse. He was six feet three in stocking feet; in boots and hat, much taller. It took a big horse to carry him—that day he rode Tequila, a fine white gelding. Dad always used a spade bit, and he had the lightest hands.

He reined in as he approached us, and Blade and I could hardly wait to tell of our great adventure. But we didn't have a chance. "What the hell do you kids think you're doing out here?" he demanded. "Just turn around and get yourselves home." He spurred his horse and was gone.

We started the long trudge home. The day was suddenly hotter. Our boots hurt and a blister burst on my heel. We were thirsty, but the thought of milk was gagging. Blade asked if I wanted a sandwich. I shook my head. "Me neither," he said.

We walked along in silence for a while and then Blade

said, "Look." I raised my eyes up from the road. "It's Mom!"

But as the station wagon approached, we realized it wasn't Mom. It was Dad. He pulled up beside us. He leaned over and opened the passenger door. He handed us cold Cokes. "I'm sorry," he said. "I didn't know you had permission."

We took the sodas and crawled into the car. I sat next to Dad. He must have gone in for lunch and taken his boots and shirt off, as he often did, before he greeted our mother. Now he wore a T-shirt and slip-on tennis shoes. His arms, never exposed to the sun, were as white as chicken skin. In the flyspecked light that blazed through the windshield, he looked bleached, inconsequential. But then he pulled me to him; I gave him a hug.

This is my father: a kindly man with lily-white arms, driving a station wagon, offering Coca-Colas and apologies. And this, too, is my father: a horseman, racing in all his fineness and his fury across an endless plain.

Mothers

My mother, around the time I was born

It is the day before Thanksgiving, and I am making bread. I haven't made bread for a long time, but I used to make it often. The four loaves I have set to rise will more than serve the ten of us who will gather in my Portland home tomorrow, my urban family of close friends, to gorge on the familiar and the nouveau: turkey with all the fixings, pears with red and yellow peppers, sun-dried-tomato salad, mincemeat pie made with venison. This feast doesn't require homemade bread—a few blocks from here I can buy chewy Tuscan bread or crisp-crusted French baguettes— but I realize, as I step back from the kneading, that the bread I make today has less to do with tomorrow than with the past.

Some mornings, if I wake and can't remember my dreaming, I curl back into the position I held during sleep, and the dream comes back. I suppose that is what this baking is all about, as well as the cigarettes I've been smoking lately, the gallons of coffee I've consumed, and the evening glasses of cheap red wine. There are memories in kneading—and in smoking and drinking—as there are in anything repetitive.

The smell of yeast takes me back to the kitchen of the house where I was raised. I have come back to the ranch for the holidays and I am kneading bread while my mother makes pies. The aluminum coffee pot murmurs on its electric trivet; the light over the table casts a warm yellow glow. I knead, my mother rolls out pie crust, we talk of everything. I can hear our voices, but I can't make out the words. Our talk is as easy and rhythmic as my kneading. We are working something around, pushing it away and pulling it to us, flipping it, flopping it, kneading with the quarter turn. We knead and knead and knead and the kneading will go on forever. The sticky parts are forgotten somewhere back in an earlier time; the kneading is what matters most. The dough finally pleases me—I hold up the great elastic ball and smack it once or twice. The sound surprises us, and we laugh. I grease the dough, plop it into the enamel wash pan, cover it with a damp cloth, set it on top of the stove to rise until I will punch it down and knead it some more. Mom finishes fluting the rims of her pies—they are perfect—and pops them into the oven. We sit down at the table and light cigarettes, she pours fresh coffee in our

mugs. And the talk continues. It will always, always continue.

But it doesn't continue. I am in my junior year of college and I have just bought a bicycle. I have made a good
deal on it, and I come back to my dorm room pleased by the
success of my Wyoming horse-trader instincts in a city like
New Haven. My roommate says: "Your father called. Your
mother is ill, terribly sick. They are taking her by ambu-
lance to Denver. He says for you to wait here by the phone."

But it isn't anything serious. It can't be anything serious.
We haven't finished kneading the bread. I fly west the next
day. In a week, my mother is dead.

The world stops for me here, and I enter a period of animal
pain. I withdraw from college, though the family insists I
must not, and I return to that ranch fifty miles from town
to help my father through the first dark months. He helps
me more than I help him, and we are both survivors. He
tends the cattle and compliments me on my cooking; I work
with a colt and begin my senior thesis. When the trees come
back in leaf, we deem ourselves fit to rejoin the human race,
and I fly east for summer term.

My mother died a dozen years ago, but I dream of her
still. In the dreams she is not dead; there is a reason she has
been gone. Briefly, I feel whole again. And then I wake.
Even now, her absence feels like a part of me cleaved away.
I have learned to compensate but there is always the dull
ache.

I have been looking for my mother these past twelve years. I have looked for her in literature, and I have looked for her in the new scholarship on women in the West. I have looked for her in my own work, in two years of interviewing that culminated in an oral history of women who worked on ranches or in the rodeo. Yet none of these books, not even my own, included my mother. She hadn't been a pioneer; she hadn't overcome poverty or extraordinary physical hardship; she didn't work outside; she was afraid of horses. Her life was not, in such identifiable ways, remarkable.

She was a typical ranch wife—supply sergeant, bookkeeper, mother, and spouse. She did the cooking, the loving, and the peacemaking. She taught me to bake bread and enjoy my height and sail out into the world with some degree of confidence. I honor these roles and yet they are just that: roles. She fulfilled them well and was proud of them, but they weren't who she *was*.

I would describe her as strong and courageous, yet these traits are not so easy to define in her as they are in my father, who crawled with a broken leg two miles down a canyon, or my Great-aunt Marie, the ranchwoman, who started riding again two months after she broke her pelvis at the age of seventy-two. My mother's proving ground was primarily within the walls of a comfortable home, a terrain both more confined and more difficult to map than my father's and my aunt's. The signposts are in those endless hours of easy conversation around our kitchen table, but I can't remember what was said. "When you talk about your father," a friend tells me, "I can see him drawn with hard, clear lines. But your mother is more like a Monet."

I don't have trouble remembering the basic details or the more obvious traits. Mom was nearly five feet eleven and she loved being tall. On the ranch she wore Levi's and, in the winter, an immense, bright-red down coat. When she went to town, she always wore four-inch heels. She was blond (usually) and slender, with an appetite for fast cars and good Scotch. An avid reader, her tastes were eclectic: Melville, Michener, Sand, Tuchman; Ayn Rand, John Fowles, Agatha Christie, *The Sensuous Woman* by J. She loved words and would pore over the Webster's *Unabridged* for hours. "Synecdoche," I remember her saying one time, sounding it out, "sin-ECK-da-key. I'll be damned. I always thought you'd say it SIN-ek-doash."

She was an effortless organizer, serving lunch to forty or fifty people after a branding; keeping the books and the payroll for the ranch; returning to college to get her teaching degree; organizing the Laramie County Cowbelles Association, an auxiliary to the Stockgrowers Association, and serving as its first president. But she was not obsessed with busyness: she liked nothing better than a good afternoon nap.

She loved to cook and I think of her most often in the kitchen, that large country kitchen with the island in the middle, counters all around, and the old oak table in front of the window. Something was always bubbling on the stove. I remember coming into the house in the winter from school or sledding or riding, tired and chilled to the bone, shucking off my coat on the back porch and then stepping across the threshold into that world of warm yellow light and heartening smells: this was home, safety, the reward for being out in the world.

I picture Mom now in that kitchen, sitting at the table after dinner. We have already done the dishes; Dad has retired, first to his recliner in the living room and then up to bed. We are drinking wine and smoking cigarettes—we have smoked nearly a pack between us. It is past midnight and breakfast will be at five-thirty. We'll have one more cigarette and then we'll go to bed. We smoke, but we're not quite ready to stop talking. We'll just finish these glasses of wine. We do. And then we light more cigarettes.

But what, oh what, did we say?

"A daughter looking at her mother's life is looking at her own," suggests poet Louise Bernikow, "shaping and fitting one life to suit the needs of another. Some have shaped monsters and some angels."

The monsters are drawn with a single stroke: When author Mary Austin's sister died, her mother said, in Mary's hearing, "Why couldn't it have been Mary?" Owen Wister's mother met his finest achievement to date, the publication of his novel *The Virginian,* with a letter in which she articulated twelve points of criticism.

The angels hardly fare better, absorbed into a faceless reverence. "They attracted little attention individually," wrote historian Dee Brown about pioneer women. "... but as a mass maternal force their power was unmatched in the domestication process that transformed the wild frontiersmen into ordinary placid citizens." The only criticism of *The Virginian* that Owen Wister accepted concerned his character Molly Wood, the "good woman" who would become the prototypic Western heroine. "I agree the heroine is the failure," he wrote home. "She seems to me without personality." "Good mothers," says a friend of mine, "are like good servants—invisible."

Are all mothers so indistinct? Bernikow talks about the "peculiar vagueness" with which we see our mothers, and Virginia Woolf, fifty years earlier, said much the same: "But if I turn to my mother," she wrote, "how difficult it is to single her out as she really was; to imagine what she was thinking, to put a single sentence into her mouth."

I drive to the beach and rent a cabin for the weekend. For eight hours a day, I set myself to the task of "free writing." The only rule is that I can't quit typing. I close my eyes and go to it, driven by a conviction, or maybe only a hope, that buried inside are the memories I need. Gradually, I am swept into greater and greater depths of recollection. My mother is constantly in view, but only occasionally can I hear her voice. At the end of the weekend I emerge, three hundred typewritten pages in hand, filled with more questions than answers. I am exhausted.

· · ·

"I don't have any more experience being a mother," Mom used to tell Blade and me, "than you have being kids." I remember these words now and think, Where did she learn? She was born Mary Jo Steele, a farmer's daughter, in Kimball, Nebraska. She had been a menopause baby, and her birth came at a devastating time for my Grandma Steele. Stricken with early and severe osteoporosis, Grandma lost seven inches of height in two years as every disc in her back disintegrated. Little Mary Jo was born into a world of pain, and also a world of resentment. "If it weren't for you," her mother would tell her, "I wouldn't be sick." Or, "If it weren't for you, we could have a new carpet." When Mary Jo was naughty, she was told, "We didn't want you anyway." She gained her height early and towered over her contemporaries. "You'd look nice," her mother would tell her, "if you weren't so skinny."

Of course, Grandma Steele also told Mary Jo she loved her. She said she lived only for her daughter's benefit.

One day when I came home from high school, Mom met me at the door. "There's a movie on tonight," she told me, "that we just have to see." It was *Now Voyager* with Bette Davis and Paul Henreid, and my mother had seen it nine times when she was in high school. "You've never seen a man so sexy as Paul Henreid," she told me. "He lights two cigarettes at a time and then hands one to Bette. He makes your heart melt."

That night we made popcorn and turned on the TV. Within moments, Mom was leaning forward in her chair, but it was not the handsome Paul Henreid that brought her to the edge of her seat. "I don't remember this," she said about Bette Davis's character, Aunt Charlotte. "How could I have forgotten?"

Charlotte is an old maid—dumpy, overweight, bespectacled—who lives with her overbearing mother, Mrs. Vale, a Philadelphia doyenne. Mrs. Vale's daughter-in-law worries about Charlotte and brings a psychiatrist to the house. Mrs. Vale denies there is anything wrong with her daughter except bad manners—Charlotte has taken to smoking and drinking to defy her—but she tells the doctor, "Charlotte was the child of my old age, my ugly duckling. All late children," she says, "are marked."

"Often," replies the psychiatrist, "they aren't wanted."

If my mother couldn't turn to her own mother as a model, she had no better luck looking to her mother-in-law. Some people say Effie Lannen married Sunny Jordan for money. If she did, she was quickly disappointed. She was a stylish woman, somewhat given to airs. She said "again" with a long *a*—"agane"—and "shan't" for "won't." ("Imagine!" my mother said once as she drove Blade and me back to the ranch after a long afternoon of Effie's grammatical corrections. "*A*gane. In Wyoming!") Effie had a genuine disdain for men who worked with their hands and no patience at all for the irregularities of ranch life. She would fly into a fury if Sunny were late for lunch. By the time my father was old enough to notice, Sunny and Effie rarely spoke to each other.

They split when Dad was ten, and Effie lived permanently in town. Because my father was the only member of his generation in either the Jordan or the Lannen families, the two clans fought through him. Pictures of him as a child show a fat little boy with the look in his eyes of someone who wanted only to please. He was sent away to military school in seventh grade, and the experience was, for him, a great escape. "At last," he recalled years later, "my world was quiet and consistent. There was no more bickering over my head."

The psychiatrist who meets Charlotte in *Now Voyager* insists that she leave home at once to recover at his clinic, Greenhaven. There, away from her mother, surrounded for the first time with nurture and support, she flourishes. At the end of her stay, the psychiatrist sends her off on an ocean voyage.

On the cruise, she meets Jerry, played by Paul Henreid, and they fall in love. He has a pet name for her, Camille. Their love is platonic—Jerry is married and must remain faithful to his wife—but together they realize a happiness new to both of them.

Jerry has to leave the cruise in Rio, but his love has empowered Charlotte; reborn as Camille, the transformation that began when she first separated from her mother is complete and she becomes the most lovely, the most fascinating, the most popular woman on the cruise.

. . .

My mother went away to college at the University of Arizona in Tucson. There she dropped the family "Mary Jo" for Jo and began to enjoy the height that had so embarrassed her in Kimball. She met my father on a blind date.

"I had been complaining that all the women I met were either too short for me or too prissy to drink," my father tells me when I ask. "One of my fraternity brothers told me he knew a woman I should meet. 'She's tall enough for you,' he said, 'and she may damn well drink you under the table.'

"There was no one minute when we realized we were violently in love," my father says about their romance. Violently: his word. "We just sort of grew together."

I suspect that early on they discussed what they wanted out of life. They had both been wounded by righteousness and martyrdom, and both their childhoods had been unhappy. They believed they didn't have to repeat their parents' mistakes. They could cash in the cards they had been dealt for new ones.

They were two ugly ducklings who had found each other.

I call up Shirley Flynn, my mother's closest friend. "Shirley," I ask, "what do you remember about Mom—not just her characteristics, but fears and aspirations. What was it like for her when Dad was laid up those two years with the broken leg that wouldn't heal? Did she ever worry about him being killed? What did she tell you about the wars that sometimes raged between Dad and Sunny?"

Shirley tells me stories Jo told her about her own mother; she says they talked sometimes about politics or religion.

"But what did Mom have to overcome on the ranch? Do you remember the time she took Blade and me to Yellowstone? I've just learned that Dad had wanted to go and Sunny forbade it. We almost left the ranch for good that time. It must have been hard for Mom—she had to have been furious with Sunny. Didn't she say anything?"

"No," Shirley answers, "she didn't say anything. Jo had such loyalty to your father—and to Sunny, too. She would never have confided in me that way."

"Sometimes Dad could be such a bastard," I say. "He'd get into one of his black moods and just retreat for days, sometimes weeks, at a time. It must have been lonely for Mom. Did she ever talk to you about it?"

"No," Shirley answers. "We didn't talk about those things."

After my folks graduated from college, my father accepted a commission in the Army and they ended up in Germany. They liked the service and Dad considered making it his career, but years of ballistics training and tank command had damaged his hearing. There was no place in the Army for a deaf officer and they decided to return to the ranch with their infant son.

My mother had become severely anemic during her first pregnancy, and she had required transfusions that kept her in the hospital for several days after my brother was born.

She was still fatigued when she learned she was pregnant again. The anemia returned and the fatigue doubled. Both parents would later remember this as the hardest period in their marriage.

Then, when I arrived, I was not the easy, happy baby that Blade had been. I was colicky; after my 2 A.M. feeding I would cry inconsolably for hours. She would walk me and walk me, and when she was so tired she couldn't walk anymore, she would set me back in my crib and close the door, go downstairs, and have a cup of coffee before she would go back to walk me some more.

"I used to sit down there and thank God I wasn't a teenage mother," she told me years later, "because at least I was mature enough to have some self-control. There were nights when all I wanted in the world was to grab you by your heels and bash your head against the wall until you quit screaming."

The railroad ran a quarter mile in front of our house and a train passed by every morning at three. There was no crossing—the tracks ran parallel to the road—but when a light shone in the kitchen, the engineer would sound his whistle.

I think of my mother sitting at the table, drinking coffee and smoking cigarettes, fifty miles from town and two miles from a neighbor, alone in the center of the night, listening to that blue whistle blow.

I rent *Now Voyager* for the weekend and find a subplot I had forgotten. Jerry has a daughter, Tina. Charlotte sees a picture of her and comments on her beauty. Jerry tells her that Tina doesn't think she's pretty; in fact, he says, "She's convinced she's an ugly duckling."

"Does she know she wasn't wanted?" asks Charlotte. Jerry admits it's true. Though his wife Isabelle is a "self-sacrificing mother," she resents Tina.

Of course, Charlotte and Tina are fated to meet. When Charlotte returns to Greenhaven for a rest, she finds Tina committed there, terribly disturbed. Tina cries during the night and Charlotte goes to her. "I'm ugly," Tina cries, "and nobody likes me. I'm not pretty in the least."

"Who ever wants that kind of prettiness?" Charlotte tells her. "There's a kind of beauty you can have if you earn it, something that has nothing to do with your face, a light that shines from inside you."

They become friends and Tina begins to flower. Tina wants a nickname for her new friend and calls her Camille. They go camping together; later, Charlotte takes the girl home with her to Philadelphia and lavishes on her all the love she never received from her own mother. "You're not like most mothers," Tina tells her. "You don't tell me what to do and what not to do all the time."

When I look to my own mother's life, it's not hard to find her Camilles. If my Grandmother Steele had been overwhelmed by the birth of her daughter, my mother nonetheless had her champions, the family members and friends who stepped in to help. There was Mom's brother Jack, nineteen years older than she, and his wife Olga. There was Mary, a surrogate aunt. And there was Mom's older sister, Clarabelle, sixteen years her senior, who filled the combined roles of mother, sister, and best friend.

And Mom would later serve as Camille herself. Clarabelle's daughter, my cousin Donna, came to the ranch nearly every summer from the time she was in junior high through college. She helped my mother with the house and with my brother and me.

"I always had such a weight problem, and my own mother would nag me all the time," Donna tells me when I call her up, "but Auntie Jo didn't. She made me feel I was pretty just the way I was. But she would have good food around the house—there was never any junk—and in the course of the summer I'd lose twenty, thirty pounds.

"I remember sitting in the bathroom," Donna tells me, "and watching your mother put on her makeup before she would go to town...."

But as Donna talks, I am back in that bathroom myself, swept up with my own memory. Mom only wore makeup when she went to town, and I loved watching her put it on. I would sit on the edge of the bathtub and watch her apply foundation, eye shadow, mascara. She would rouge her cheeks, put on lipstick and perfume. That night she and my father were going to a party and she wore a sundress of iridescent green silk. She was humming to herself as she finished her makeup. She looked one more time in the mirror and smiled the hugest smile. Then she turned to me, fluttered her eyelashes theatrically, laughed. She picked me up, swung me around. "I feel pretty," she sang from *West Side Story* as we danced out into the hall,

"Oh so pretty and witty and gay, and I pity anyone who isn't me today...."

"Larry, I just have to get out of here."

I never heard my mother speak these words; my father quotes them to me now. We are talking about the winter my mother went to Mexico with her sister Clarabelle. A blizzard blew in right after she left and dumped several feet of snow; then the sun came out. We were calving, and Dad needed to be out in the glare all day. He sunburns badly; in the days before sunblock he would stop shaving for a few days and draw black circles of burned cork around his eyes, his nose, his mouth. He looked fierce and wonderful. Blade and I called him the bogey man and pleaded with him to draw cork around our eyes, too.

I came down with the flu and spent nearly two weeks in bed with a basin close by. My illness didn't seem to faze my father. He would come in every couple of hours in his layers of insulated clothing and his bogey-man face, bringing me saltines and a fresh glass of 7-Up. He'd sit on the edge of the Hide-A-Bed in the living room, take my temperature, play a hand of cribbage, or just talk for a few minutes. He gave me antibiotics—every rancher knows which vet medicines can be used on humans, and Dad made a big production out of weighing me like a calf and then cutting up a cow bolus as big as his thumb into fractions suitable to my weight. I felt entirely pampered.

"Do you ever worry that Jo isn't coming back?" a neighbor asked over drinks one night.

"No," my father answered. "She said she would and she will. If she wasn't going to, she would have told me."

One summer, I wanted to learn to make bread. Mom and I pulled out various flours—wheat, white, rye, cornmeal— and she showed me how to make a sponge with the yeast, honey, warm water, and dry milk. "Let it rise for a little bit, then add half the flour and let it rise again for an hour or so. The yeast gets a better start without salt or oil. Put those in when you add the second half of the flour. But if you don't have time for all this, just put everything in together. There's really nothing you can do to hurt bread," Mom told me. "Use what you have on hand. Just keep working it around until it feels right."

"Did your mother teach you to make bread?" I asked.

"You know, it's funny—I really don't know where I learned. By the seat of my pants, I guess."

When I was eight years old, I got my first young horse, a green-broke four-year-old gelding. He was a Quarter Horse–Arabian cross, sorrel with four white stockings and a perfect blaze. The graduation from old nag to "real" horse is an important rite of passage for any ranch kid, and I was terribly proud; I thought mine was the most beautiful horse in the world and I named him G.B. for Golden Beauty.

G.B. was spirited and he liked to buck. He tossed me a couple of times, but I was sure I could handle him. Then he threw me on my head and knocked me senseless. I still have no memory of the first part of that day, though I'm told I got back on and rode home with my friends, the Vineyard boys, who lived on the upper end of the ranch. Mrs. Vineyard took me into the doctor—my own mother had gone to town earlier for groceries—and when I came to my senses in the doctor's office several hours later, Mom was by my side. The doctor, after one more conversation, could see no reason to keep me overnight and we headed back to the ranch.

It was dark out and I lay down on the front seat with my head on Mom's lap. I remember the glow of the dials on the dashboard. "Before today," she said as we sped along that road she knew so well, "I never thought what it would be like to lose one of you. For a while, I didn't know if you'd come back."

I remember the touch of her hand on my hair.

"How are you feeling," she asked.

"Fine," I answered. She touched the moisture away from my cheek, and then from her own.

The next day, we were supposed to move cattle, and I didn't want to go. My head didn't hurt, my eyes were the same size, but I said I felt sick to my stomach. The day after that, I didn't feel any better. On the third day, I still didn't want to ride and Dad confronted me. "Is it G.B.?" Dad asked. "Are you afraid of him?"

"I'm not afraid. I just don't feel good."

And I sulked out of the room.

That night, Mom came in to tuck me in. She asked me how I was. "Fine," I said.

"How do you feel about G.B.," she asked me.

"Fine. He's my horse. I love him."

"Honey," she said, "he may be too much horse for you right now. There's no disgrace in that. He's a lot of horse for someone as young as you."

"I'm not scared of him. I just don't feel good."

"Honey," she said, "if you *are* scared, he'll sense it. And you'll get hurt again."

"I'm not scared," I said.

"If you won't want to ride him, it's okay. We'll do something about another horse. But you've got to tell us."

"I'm not scared."

Mom was quiet for a while. "You know," she said, "you are a very good rider. I've been watching you, and you get better every day." I didn't say anything. "You're really good with horses," she added. "You know?"

"I know," I said begrudgingly.

But in the morning, something was different. We were supposed to ride and I didn't try to get out of it. I *was* afraid when I first stepped on G.B., but after I'd ridden a few minutes, I wasn't afraid anymore.

I might have been afraid forever.

The part my mother liked best about baking was kneading the dough. "You haven't been to the ocean yet," she told me the first time we made bread together, "but when you walk along the edge of the water, the surf washes back and forth over your feet and it's the most soothing thing in the world. It just washes all your tensions away. Kneading is like that."

I remember watching the strength in her hands, listening to the rhythm of the push-fold-turn. "You can't knead bread too much," she was saying. "The more you work it, the finer the grain. It starts out being sticky and rough, but just keep kneading and gradually it becomes smoother and more elastic, it grows cooler to the touch. It's like something alive. Look at it now," she said as she ran her hand lovingly over the big ball of dough. "It's as smooth as a baby's bottom."

"Don't you ever get lonely out here?" I asked my mother one time.

"Oh sure," she answered. "Don't you?"

"Yeah," I said, "I guess sometimes I do."

"You know, when you were little and I'd be sitting at this table in the middle of the night and hear that train whistle blow, I used to think that things couldn't get any lonelier than that. But one night I got to thinking. If we were living in town, I wouldn't even have a train to say hello to."

One summer my mother went over to the University in Laramie and earned her teaching degree. My brother was just about to finish sixth grade—the last year offered in the one-room school at Iron Mountain. Like most families in such isolated circumstances, we had several options. Blade could take the bus to school in Cheyenne every day, a four-hour round trip. Mom could move to town and take us with her. Or we could go to boarding school. My parents thought the bus trip too hard, and they didn't want to split up for the next eight school years to see the two of us through graduation. The Iron Mountain school was in need of a teacher; if Mom taught, we could afford boarding school. Blade went away to Kansas and later to New Mexico; I went to Iowa and Colorado.

When I talk about my life, I say boarding school gave me confidence. But I'm hiding something here. If I eventually developed a degree of self-assurance, my first two years were miserable. Both my brother and I were scared little kids with no more social skills than weanling calves, painfully easy targets for ridicule and hazing. We were just so tender. *How could she bear to send us away?*

Every mother must constantly choose between her children and her spouse. On the ranch, the choice was just more obvious. My parents never tried to obscure the fact it *was* a choice; they never told us they did it solely because they loved us. They did love us and we knew it. But they chose to stay with each other.

I reached puberty in my eighth-grade year, and when I came home that summer, I had changed from a chunky little kid into a willowy teenager. My mother met the changes in me with a sense of delight. Our deeper closeness began then. I believe this came in part from the fact that she was at ease with her own sexuality and not threatened by mine, but I also know that she had faith in transformation. She had cut her teeth on Bette Davis's, she had engineered her own, she had participated in my cousin Donna's. That I could be emerging into a reasonably attractive and well-rounded young woman must have reassured her that I could survive the choices she had made.

In my sophomore year, my brother and I came back to Cheyenne for high school. Our family bought a trailer house in town and Mom stayed with us during the week and went back to the ranch on weekends.

There were times during those years when I hated her. They were fleeting moments of rage, pure and frightening. When I was in one of my moods, anything could set me off —a comment about my hair, a request I help with the dishes. Though I know these outbursts hurt her, she simply let them pass; they didn't escalate into something unbreachable between us. I felt I could talk to her about anything: boys, sex, skiing, my debate case, my hopes for college. My friends gathered around her; she was the person they came to when they had trouble at home. She wasn't like other mothers, they told me. She could step into their world.

She *wasn't* like other mothers. One day at Civic League, each member had been asked to stand up and say a few words about herself. One woman, whose son was president of his high school class and captain of the football team, stood up and described herself, simply and completely, as "David's mother." "What does she read?" my mother asked that night at dinner when she told the story. "What does she think? What does she have that's *hers*?"

. . .

"You do so many things well," I said to her one time. "Haven't you ever wanted to have your own career?"

"I have my own career," she answered, "right here, with your father."

"That's *his* career," I said.

"No," she told me, "you don't understand. This is *our* career. This is something we've done together. And you can't imagine how satisfying this work has been." She gestured then, the sweep of her hand taking in the kitchen, the house, my father sleeping upstairs, the whole of that ranch that had occupied her for a quarter of a century fifty miles from town.

I thought she was naïve. I had come home from college armed with books by Betty Friedan and Germaine Greer. But she was right. I *didn't* understand. I didn't understand her life and I didn't understand the authors I was reading.

My mother was living a life that fulfilled her. She had chosen to be a wife and a mother, but she had also chosen to be a full-fledged business partner in the family corporation. I don't know what her life would have been like had we lived in town and Dad gone "out" to work each day while she stayed "home," but a ranch is closer to the preindustrial model in which home, family, and work are inseparable.

If my parents' division of labor was fairly conventional, it was also true to their individual likes and talents. Mom didn't enjoy large animals, machinery, or extreme physical labor; Dad didn't like detail work. He managed the ranch and worked outside; she administered it, keeping the books and procuring supplies. They shared child care to a significant degree, at least from the time Blade and I were five or six and could ride. If we were shorthanded, Mom drove a piece of haying equipment; if she were overly tired or running behind schedule, Dad would pick up the vacuum cleaner or treat us to his famous fried-egg sandwiches. They made decisions together and it was never "his ranch" or "his money," it was "theirs." Although most family agriculture follows this model in theory, I've come to appreciate how rare was the full measure of respect my parents afforded each other.

I believe my mother found satisfaction in these roles of wife, mother, and business partner, but she had chosen, as well, to be something bigger and more complex than any of them: she had chosen to be fully herself. Early on, she had decided not to make sacrifices she couldn't make willingly; from that authentic core, she was able to marry and mother free of martyrdom or guilt.

"That winter your mother told me she wanted to leave," my father tells me, "I didn't resent it, and I wasn't afraid. I didn't understand why she needed to go, but if she said it was important, I could accept it.

"Jo was absolutely and without doubt my best friend. Yet there was some area deep inside each of us that was foreign to the other. That sounds like a contradiction, and I suppose it is. But both things are true."

I suspect, if Mom were alive, she would have said much the same. I remember the summer after I graduated from high school when Dad was deep in one of his black moods.

He was not intentionally mean in these moods, just lost in a vague and simmering anger. "Mom," I said, "how do you stand it?"

"I know who he *is*," she answered. "He isn't that person right now, but he will be again."

For my junior year of college, I transferred from Colorado State to Yale. I marched off to the Ivy League with a set of orange Samsonite suitcases and a sophisticated vocabulary that included words like "golly" and "gees McGees." I remember my first breakfast in the dining hall. Two young men at my table were speaking in heavy English accents and I asked them where they were from.

"The Bronx," answered one.

"New Jersey," said the other.

Two thoughts entered my mind at exactly the same moment. The first was a vow that I would not leave that place talking like an Englishman. The second was the sudden knowledge that I'd gotten in way over my head.

My first semester was miserable. I felt lonely and outclassed. Gradually, I learned my way around and began to make friends, but I knew I was headed for disaster. "If you got in, you can make it through," my roommate assured me, but I didn't believe her. Finals were a nightmare. I don't know how I completed the term.

I couldn't wait to be back in Wyoming for the holiday, riding, baking, catching up on my sleep. A blizzard blew in over New Year's and my boyfriend and I spent four days snowed in with my parents. We read and drank and talked and played poker. I was not happy to see the skies clear and the vacation come to an end.

The night before I left, Mom came into my room and sat on the edge of my bed. We talked for a while, and then she said, "What's wrong? You've been edgy all day." It all came out then, my fears about going back to school. I was worried I hadn't done well in my classes; I didn't fit in; I wasn't smart enough. I should go back to Colorado State. But Mom was simply reassuring: it took a while to settle into things. Surely everyone felt the same way when they arrived as freshmen; as a transfer student, I just had less company in my adjustment. Even if I hadn't done as well first term as I'd like, she told me, I'd figure it out. "You always have before," she said.

I was still worried when she left my room, but I slept well that night. The next day I was packed early, ready to go.

Mom and I often discussed the things that were important to us, our passions, our fears. She never put much truck into worrying about the future. When something bad happened, she believed, you just took care of it. But one fear engaged her. She worried that an accident or old age might leave her a vegetable, a body without intelligence or spirit. This is a common fear—I certainly share it—but it always surprised me that she mentioned it so often. Only now do I begin to understand. She had created her life as a matter of choice and a triumph of will. How frightening it must have been to consider losing that ability.

My mother's headaches started when I was in high school. They were severe, but so occasional she didn't worry about them much. Between high school and college, I went to New Zealand for a year. By the time I came home, the headaches had worsened and she was undergoing rigorous tests. The doctors in Cheyenne could find nothing wrong.

The headaches became more severe and lasted longer. Sometimes they were literally blinding. She went back for more tests, and then the doctors sent her to the Mayo Clinic. More tests. Still, they could find nothing physically wrong. They suggested tension as the cause—her last child was entering college, about to leave home for good. "Empty nest syndrome" was a diagnosis in vogue at the time. They moved her to the psychiatric ward, taught her biofeedback, hypnotized her, gave her stress tapes. And then they sent her home.

She learned to meditate. She listened to her stress tapes every day. The methods helped her manage the pain, but they didn't make it go away. "If you outlive me," she told us, "you have them cut me open. Something's got to be physically wrong in there. I just don't think I'm all that unhappy."

. . .

Shortly after my parents' twenty-fifth anniversary, my mother suffered an aneurysm. By the time I arrived at the hospital in Denver where she had been taken, she had undergone surgery to remove a blood clot the size of a grapefruit from her brain. She had lost her speech center and was entirely paralyzed on one side, partially paralyzed on the other. We could visit her in the intensive care unit only ten minutes out of every hour. She was usually awake, and she would hold one of our hands. We would talk to her, tell her where she was, what had happened. We told her that the doctors had found evidence of earlier aneurysms—the pressure from their clotting had caused her headaches all along. We would ask her to squeeze if she understood what we were saying, and sometimes she did.

I remembered our conversation at Christmas, and I was afraid she would be worried about me. I told her that I had returned to school and she had been right. I had done fine in my classes. Everything that had seemed so alien and hard that first semester was easier now. She squeezed my hand.

When we came out of the ICU, my father asked me about what I had said to her. "Were you having trouble?"

"No, Dad, it was just something Mom and I talked about when I was home."

In a few days, she was moved from the ICU. Because of the extent of her brain damage, she had little chance for significant long-term recovery, but she was off the critical list.

A couple of days later, her brain started to spasm. The doctors didn't know why—it was something that occasionally followed an aneurysm. Sometimes, they said, it seemed to be almost a matter of will. It was usually fatal.

At four o'clock that afternoon, my mother died.

I am back in the kitchen again, baking bread. I find myself thinking about a story I heard recently from a lecture by photographer Duane Michals. When he was a boy, his father told him that he would write him a letter in which he explained things. Michals was to have it on his father's death. He treasured the thought of the letter all the time he was growing up; his father died without ever writing it. The story gave me goose bumps; even now it haunts me. Don't we all believe, at some level, that our elders know something they will someday reveal? And how many of us go to our graves without ever knowing what it was, without ever passing it on to our own children?

I believe that my mother tried to tell me the truth, as much as she knew it at the time and as much as she was able. The truth wasn't always easy to take, but I have not had to reconcile the difference between what I was told with what, on a deeper level, I knew.

And I think it is this fear of the truth that keeps us vague about our mothers. Children need fairy tales because they can see only black and white. The wicked stepmother pairs off against Cinderella to let children rail symbolically against the "bad mother" who scolds them while not losing the "good mother" who loves and protects them. As adults, we are supposed to be able to accept both sides, but I wonder how successfully we do. "Bad" mothers are obliterated with a few black words; "good" mothers pale in the light of their haloes. Lest we see detail that might overwhelm us, we don't look closely at all.

When we give up fairy tales, we take a vow of silence. It's not easy to break that vow, but I am becoming confident in my mother's ability to stand in the light and I feel strong enough to join her there. I'm also getting used to hearing her voice. About the myth that keeps mothers and daughters lying to each other—lying *about* each other—she comes in loud and clear: "That's dumb."

If she couldn't give me everything I wanted, she gave me enough to make me feel safe. She was the one person to whom I could admit my fears, and she helped me work them around until they no longer frightened me. This was something she had learned to do for herself; it was something I was learning when she died. It is what I miss most now; it is what I am looking for as I knead this bread. No other reassurance has ever felt like hers because no one else has ever known what it takes to make a loaf of bread this good.

Now I have to confront how scared I am to go on alone. "It's all right," she would tell me. "I've been watching you. You're getting better every day."

How Coyote Sent
the White Girl Home

Me in our front yard

Before I tell you how Coyote sent the white girl home, I must tell you how she became ashamed of her homeland. I can remember the exact moment. I was ten years old, just entering sixth grade. I had outgrown the one-room school at Iron Mountain, and I went to live with a family in town. I shared a room with the daughter, Laurie, an eighth-grader. Laurie was deliciously sophisticated, the big sister I had always wanted. Self-assured and beautiful, she had matching bedroom furniture and wore nylons and a bra.

The first night, intoxicated by the excitement of moving in, we stayed awake late, talking in the darkness while Top 40 music played on the white plastic clock radio. "What sort of music do you like?" Laurie asked me.

"What do you mean, what sort?" At home we listened to KLZ out of Denver, a middle-of-the road station that provided us with weather and farm reports and played Frank Sinatra and Roger Williams. We had a hi-fi, too, and my folks' tastes ranged from gunfighter ballads to opera. I knew classical music was a "type," but I had always grouped most other music together.

"You know," Laurie said. "Rock and roll, folk, jazz, classical, country and western."

"Oh," I said. "I must like country and western. I'm from the country."

"That's queer," Laurie said. "Only queers like country and western."

"What's a queer?" I asked.

"Oh God," Laurie said. "I have my work cut out for me."

In that moment, I experienced my first shame of place and perpetrated my first betrayal. The shame was not great, nor was the betrayal—who has traversed adolescence without begging to be picked up on the corner so our friends wouldn't discover that we had parents? Much of this is no more than a healthy move toward individuation. But this moment stands out for me as the first time I realized that success in the larger, more sophisticated world meant abandoning values I had learned at home.

If I had intended to return home, I might have found a way to bridge the gap. But already, at the age of ten, I did *not* intend to return. From as far back as I can remember, when family discussion ran to what I would be when I grew up, ranching was never considered. My father believed

I had an acumen for business; he imagined me as the CEO of a large firm. My mother thought I might find my place as an academic or a foreign correspondent. I realize now that my folks already knew they would sell the ranch once my grandfather died, but I suspect they would have prepared me to make my way in the larger world regardless. They were white, middle-class, and educated. They respected the professions and operated on the assumption—so basic to their class that it was virtually invisible—that my fullest realization would be through professional work. They were preparing me for success. And they were preparing me, though they didn't realize it, to abandon them.

During that first year in Cheyenne, my sixth-grade English teacher asked us to write about something unusual. I told about finding a skunk, a porcupine, and a raccoon in separate stalls in the barn one night. One of the other kids said it was a stupid thing to write about, but the teacher came to my defense—the student was just jealous, she said, because he didn't have anything special to write about. Special—the word felt like a slap. I swore to myself then, with the earnestness only a sixth-grader can muster, that I would never be branded "special" again. If country and western was "queer" or country anything was "special," I would bury the rural as deep as I could.

By the next year, when I started boarding school, my shame was well entrenched. On Parents' Day, the other girls' families would pull up in their Lincoln Mark IVs and their BMWs, the fathers handsome in their three-piece suits and their polished shoes, the women elegant in their long fur coats. And then my parents would arrive in their red, mud-splattered station wagon. My father would step out in his boots and tall Stetson hat, my mother in her cloth coat. No difference that they were taller and more striking and at least as confident as the other parents; all I could see was their hickishness, their boorishness, their poverty. How queer they were, those rubes from the country who acted like they knew me. How much I wanted to die.

I'd like to think that my shame was a product purely of adolescence and my own insecurity, but there was something deep and cultural to it, a subtle but pervasive contempt not only for the rural but for anything small or local. When I returned to Cheyenne for high school, I recognized it among my more ambitious classmates. We were the bright kids in the accelerated English classes, and already Cheyenne seemed like too small a place. Our success seemed tied to how completely we severed the ties with home. We read of Hemingway's comment about his midwestern hometown—a place, he reputedly said, of broad lawns and narrow minds—and we snickered with recognition. If happiness was Lubbock, Texas, in the rearview mirror, as one popular song had it, ecstasy was Cheyenne a few thousand miles away.

With maturity, most of us have come to profess a certain fondness for Cheyenne, but the shame—or, more accurately, the assumption of our carefully educated superiority—is still there in subtle ways. I attended a high-school friend's wedding in Washington, D.C., and found that her friends and colleagues, mostly high-level government employees like herself, were surprised to learn that her family was from Wyoming. Such a basic fact is not simply overlooked among close friends, it is hidden—after all, her friends knew where she had earned her degrees. By that time I had turned back to my roots with a fierce protectiveness. I was quick to judge, but my response was false, a projection of my own betrayal.

I don't question my desire for education—I can't imagine it otherwise. But I do question the inevitable course that education seemed to dictate, as if it could have no application within the community that bred me, as if it would be wasted were I to return.

In my earliest memory, I am standing at the screen door, watching someone leave. I am just old enough to walk; I can't reach the latch. I don't remember who is leaving and the sun is so bright I can't see past its glare. I remember heat radiating off the sidewalk and white sheets hanging lifeless on the line. I remember globs of green paint dried in tiny squares along the edges of the screen. I remember the line of pole fence that marks the perimeter of the yard and how its red paint is faded and peeling. I remember how the world beyond that fence seems brilliant and mysterious. I cry and cry. I want to go, too.

I have another memory, perhaps from the same summer. It is dusk and my mother, my brother, and I are returning to the ranch from town. When we top the hill that gives us our first view of home, we search out the light in the yard, as we always do, for comfort. But tonight we gain the vantage point just as a blood-red moon rises behind the buildings. Perhaps there are forest fires further north;

whatever the cause, the moon is so red and so bright that I think our house is in flames. I burst into tears. I want to be home.

That child in me that yearned to venture forth into the brilliant and mysterious world has always been rewarded. But the child that wanted to come home makes me feel ashamed. I once admitted to a family friend that I yearned to find a way to return to agriculture. "Heavens," she said, "haven't you outgrown that ranch thing yet?" For years, this was my shame. There was something wrong with me. I couldn't outgrow that ranch thing. Only now do I ask: why was it always assumed that I should?

Thomas Jefferson thought of education as a gift. A person would leave home to become educated and then return with the gift of that learning. The new knowledge would benefit the community and the student would continue to receive from that community the deeper, older education of place. It was an exchange that went both ways. A classically educated person would learn from the great literature of the world and also from the land.

But we tend to think of education more as a commodity, as something that we buy and pay for and consequently own, something that does not carry obligation but rather releases us from it. We tend, too, to value a person not for what she knows through experience in the world or through self-directed study, but for what she has learned in the sanctified halls of learning, her professional credentials.

Education, which Jefferson hoped would strengthen the

bond with home, more often tends to sever it. In a 1978 article in *Esquire* magazine titled "The Dangerous Arrogance of the New Elite," the attorney David Lebedoff noted the increasing polarization of Americans into two groups, which he deemed the New Elite, or highly educated, and the Left Behinds, or everybody else. "It is impossible to exaggerate how insular this new class is," he wrote of the New Elite. "Its members talk only to one another. . . . Once [they] are off the campuses they usually work and live only with one another. . . . They have no idea what the rest of the country is like." Lebedoff's division was exaggerated and yet it rings true. The saying that "you can't go home again" carries the weight of American gospel.

I think about the generations of landscape and lore that have shaped me and I'm struck by a curious thought. I'm the fourth generation that tried to leave the land and kept some tie to it only through tragedy, failure, or default. My great-grandfather tried repeatedly to sell the ranch but couldn't get the job done. My grandfather wanted to be a banker and both he and his father invested in a Cheyenne bank to make it possible, but the Great Depression came along and the bank failed. My own father would have built a career in the Army if he hadn't gone deaf. And I would now be a journalist living in Mexico City or Managua if my mother hadn't died while I was in college.

When I withdrew for a semester to spend time with my father, I began work on my senior thesis. I was taking my degree in Latin American studies, but I couldn't research a

Mexican subject in Cheyenne (I had planned to look into the press coverage of the massacre of students in Mexico City before the 1968 Olympics). My advisor suggested I choose a Wyoming topic and I decided to focus on the experience of ranchers during the agricultural depression of the 1920s and 1930s.

Every day, I drove the pickup into Cheyenne to work in the State Archives. I pored over newspapers, livestock reports, reminiscences, and memoirs—anything I could find. At first, the work was a diversion, something to distract me from my overwhelming grief. But gradually a sense of excitement began to sink in. This was it. This made sense. In the midst of those dark days, I often found myself blinded with recognition. My mother was dead and the ranch was for sale, but in the study of the American West, I had found a way to come home.

Coyote, that old trickster, is the master of disguises, the emperor of irony, "the great culture bringer who can also make mischief beyond belief." I said I would explain how he sent the white girl home, and the tale is quick to tell. My personal Coyote comes in the guise of education. Education has given me a road back to my people, but it has also kept me apart.

Several years ago, I went camping in eastern Oregon with friends. We all lived in the city; I was the only one who hadn't been born there. We were hiking in the desert one morning and came across a rattlesnake. I picked up a handful of rocks and stoned it to death, then took the rattle.

My action had been automatic, almost like swatting a mosquito, but my friends were aghast. How could I kill that snake? It was part of the ecosystem. It wasn't hurting us.

I became defensive. It was easy for my urban friends to feel friendly toward rattlesnakes because they had never lived around them. Would they feel the same toward sewer rats? What about all those pigeons the city poisons every day?

Where I was raised, rattlesnakes are a threat, and you kill them when you see them. Bull snakes are good. They keep the rodent population under control and you do everything in your power to protect them. But rattlesnakes are bad—they are poisonous. We often had horses and cows bit by rattlesnakes; through the years we lost dozens of dogs and cats. Just about everybody who lives in rattlesnake country has been dumped off a horse frightened by a rattlesnake. (Interestingly enough, people rarely get bitten. In my family's ninety-year tenure at Iron Mountain, an area famous for the size and quantity of its rattlesnakes, only one person was bitten on our ranch.) But there is also little hysteria about snakes. You watch for them; if you see one, you kill it. The killing probably has a lot to do with the absence of hysteria. It gives the illusion of control. Some things don't need a lot of thought. You're never going to eradicate the rattlesnake. It is not now and never will be an endangered species. Can't *anything* just be black and white?

Yes, but what does one snake matter in the scale of the whole? And if it doesn't matter, why kill it?

Well, figure a female snake has a dozen young each year. Half of them are female and they will have six daughters a year. If all the snakes live, in a decade the original mother will have over 33,000 descendants. It matters if you kill a snake.

But think how many mice 33,000 snakes kill a year. It *does* matter if you kill a single snake.

And, of course, in the life cycle of snakes in this vast, uninhabited quarter, man has little impact compared to the daily commerce of hawks and eagles and disease and the even more important ebb and flow of rodents to feed on.

But the snake-killing episode has disturbed me. Why *did* I kill that snake? Because I come from snake-killing people. Does it make sense to kill snakes? There, on the open desert, no. Does it ever make sense to kill snakes? Yes —around the buildings, around the corrals, around watering holes. Does it always make sense to kill snakes? No. Will I kill another snake? Not thoughtlessly. But can I go home again with a different attitude about killing snakes? Ahh, that's the problem.

My new life and my old one are at odds. I seem to need to leave one set of people or the other. It is easier to simply agree that my new friends are right, there is no reason to kill snakes and how brutish and dull to do so in the first place. It is more difficult to accept that part of me that comes from snake-killing people, and to make peace with it. It is hardest of all to find a way to open a discussion about snake killing in my original community or to pass on some genuine understanding about that community to my new friends.

My education can insulate me from this dilemma, for it suggests that I learn *about* the West rather than *from* its people. The library would keep me safe if I would let it. But I miss my people too much. They have too much to teach me. They have too much to teach my new friends. The knowledge they have is neither quaint nor Left Behind. I need to find a way to continue to learn from it. I need to pass it on.

When I left for my senior year of college, the ranch had been sold and the new owner was due to take possession in a few weeks. A short while later, my father called, disgruntled. The sale had fallen through. I offered him sympathy, but I felt like I'd been granted a reprieve. As soon as I graduated that spring, I headed home. By that time, another deal had been struck. The summer would be my last chance to work on the ranch.

We were in the third year of a desperate drought. We had received no moisture for over a year and had cut our cow herd down to half its normal size so as not to damage the land. When I worked on my senior thesis, I had interviewed ranchers who had lived through the unrelenting drought of the thirties. The head of the Warren Livestock Company told me that the ground was so bare you could drop a dime and find it a week later. My Great-aunt Marie told me that some cattle were so starved down they had to be killed in the fields. I quoted Struthers Burt from *Powder River: Let 'er Buck:* "Drought is like a dying woman, wide eyed, staring, never moving, fever on her lips." I thought I knew something about drought but nothing prepared me for that summer.

It was not just the dryness of the land, the sparseness of feed. A malaise hung over everything and our cattle were sick. We had coccidiosis in our calves, a viral diarrhea that, untreated, made them literally shit themselves to death. All summer long, as the men put up what little hay grew in the meadows, I rode and doctored calves. Each morning, I saddled up, headed out to one of the pastures where we kept cows and calves, and rode the herd.

When I found a sick calf, I would rope it, wrestle it to the ground, and hog-tie it, and then give it a couple of large boluses called Spanbolets and inject it with antibiotic. In my saddlebags, I carried cattle markers, large grease sticks in half a dozen colors, and I would mark each calf after I treated it—a red circle around the right eye one day, a yellow line down the front of the face the next. Many calves I doctored so many times I had no more room for grease-paint. Each day, one or two died. Sometimes so many were sick I needed help, and our foreman Leonard Cheser or his son Dan would join me—they didn't have enough hay to keep them busy, anyway. Coccidiosis causes a particularly foul diarrhea, a smell that you never forget, something that doesn't come off in the bath.

Then both herds of our horses came down with dust pneumonia. We had no way to doctor calves except on horseback. Neighbors lent us more horses. We kept them quarantined and prayed for their health.

On the twenty-second of July, I woke to my father's shout: "It's raining!" I found him outside in his BVDs and T-shirt, arms outstretched to the sky. "Oh thank you,

Lord," he yelled. "Not for me, because I've seen rain before. But for the *children.*"

I walked out into the horse pasture to catch my day's mount. All summer long, I had walked up to whatever horse I wanted, but that day the horses were wild with the weather and took off running the moment they saw me, kicking and bucking and squealing. I chased them around the square-mile pasture three times before I caught one. I came back to the barn to find Leonard and Dan arm in arm, singing "Ninety-nine Bottles of Beer on the Wall" like a couple of high-school drunks. They *were* drunk: on water rather than whiskey.

By the time I reached the J T pasture to start my day's work, fog had set in. I doctored a couple of calves near the windmill, but most of the cattle had moved up to higher ground. I rode up the breaks, but by the time I reached the top, I couldn't see sagebrush ten feet in front of me, so I turned around. As I rode back down the draw, I heard footsteps behind me. Two dozen cows and calves, running as hard as they could, emerged from the mist and raced past, kicking and cavorting, only to disappear again into the fog. Two more bunches ran past. My horse wanted his head so I gave it to him. We raced with a blind abandon and I found myself laughing out loud.

Within hours, the grass started to green. The earth is so anxious for its pleasure, so grateful in return. The drought had broken; it rained for several days. And in just a few weeks my family moved off the land forever.

When my family tells the story of the ranch, we say we

left because we had to—we could not afford to pay the estate taxes after my grandfather's death. This is true, but it is only part of the story. My family left the land because for four generations we had yearned to leave. We had lived in a culture that taught us that a professional life is more respectable than one tied to the land. This attitude shaped the decisions my family made, and it continues to shape the larger political and economic decisions, made by educators and policymakers far removed from the land, that affect the few who still hold on.

My sadness over the loss of the homeplace is my dark side, my grief, but it is also the source of my deepest knowledge. Perhaps it is only through this experience of loss that I can value a sense of place, that I can question how thoughtlessly—even how contemptuously—we are taught to cast it aside.

Newtime

A Calving Diary

March 29: The windchill dipped below zero this morning and Charlie and I found a cold calf up the Big Hill. We could see that something was wrong from a long way off—a healthy calf curls up in a ball against the wind but a chilled one lays out flat. This one was almost dead, its eyes blue and rolled up in its head. We lifted it up into my saddle and it was so limp it didn't seem to have bones. Charlie trailed the cow down while I carried the calf; the poor little thing was so cold it couldn't even shiver. I rubbed its fur as I rode. It didn't seem to have any heat in its body at all, but once or twice it gave a little jerk and I knew it was still alive. I found myself talking to it, telling it what a fine calf it was, how big and how strong. The

wind sucked away any warmth the two of us could gen-
erate and I held the calf more tightly. It was hard not to
feel sentimental. All right, I did feel sentimental. But
nothing else I do is this simple, this satisfying. Nothing else
is this vital.

The Farthing Ranch borders the ranch where I was
raised. Charlie Farthing is my oldest friend. He and I were
born two days apart in the same hospital and call each other
littermates. We went to the one-room school at Iron Mountain together. Now he and his wife Carol ranch with their
three children—Chris, Tom, and Ryan, ages six, four, and
two—and Charlie's father, Merrill, age eighty-six. They are
like family to me, a connection not by progeny but by prox-
imity, as close a tie out here in this vast arid land as genetics.

A few weeks ago I called to see if I could join them for
calving season. "Why would you want to come then?" they
asked. "It's so hectic around here. Everyone is exhausted
and bad-tempered."

Calving is the crux point of the year and it is something
I have never experienced. By the time I was old enough to
be useful, I left for boarding school. I was never home in
the spring. I have seen calves born. I have assisted in a few
births. But I have never been there for the season, for the
grueling week after week of incessant emergency and response.

Merrill's father came from New York in 1903 and
started this ranch with two thousand acres. Now, though
Farthings are modest folk, Merrill speaks of the ranch in
townships rather than acres or sections. A section, a square

mile, is six hundred and forty acres. A township is thirty-six sections. On close to three townships, Farthings run about eight hundred head of mother cows. They also run yearlings and two-year-old-heifers. Unlike many ranchers, they don't calve out two-year-olds. A two-year-old heifer is like a fourteen-year-old girl, physically able to have a baby but not mature enough to do it easily. The Farthings run this large outfit with very little help. Merrill, Charlie, Carol, and Cory, the hired hand, do all the work. Calving two-year-olds is labor intensive and the Farthings figure it makes more sense to carry them over another year before they're bred.

At eighty-six, Merrill is thin and wiry and leather-skinned; he works long days and jokes about his age. "If I'd known I was going to live this long," he says, "I'd have taken better care of myself." He also says that he'd like to jack up his head and run a new body under it. Grayce, his wife of over half a century, died three years ago, and Merrill has just started to date again. He is particularly sweet on a woman named Maxine but has a rival for her affection, a doctor and long-time friend. "He's younger, smarter, and better-looking than I am," Merrill says, "and he drives a thirty-seven-thousand-dollar Cadillac. I don't know what she sees in him." Merrill drives a GMC pickup and we help him wash it each Saturday afternoon before he heads to town for his weekly date.

Charlie looks almost exactly like Prince Charles—or, as Charlie insists, Prince Charles looks like Charlie Farthing. Tall and thin and restless, he has, to use Merrill's term, an omnivorous appetite. I have seen him consume four pork chops and eight potatoes at a single sitting. The pork chops serve, I suspect, as an excuse for the potatoes. Charlie eats so many potatoes that Carol has developed an allergy from peeling them. Once he grew a mustache and Carol objected: imagine Prince Charles with a pencil-thin mustache. She begged and pleaded, joked and cajoled, but the whiskers remained. Then she threatened to stop cooking potatoes; fifteen minutes later Charlie emerged from the bathroom clean-shaven.

A town girl and accomplished horsewoman when she met Charlie, Carol has degrees in teaching and music but prefers ranching to either. She and Charlie worked side by side until they started their family. Now her horseback days are limited until all three boys can ride, but she handles just about every job imaginable from her Suburban, a 4X4 station wagon on a pickup chassis. Unflappable and indefatigable, she meets crisis with a deep-bellied laugh and wishes she could have a dozen more children.

Twenty-three-year-old Cory Everett and his wife Jennifer came to the ranch three months ago from southern Colorado. Neither has lived this far from town before. Cory grew up on a ranch and loves the work; Jennifer isn't so sure about the isolation but hopes to get a job as postmaster at Horse Creek, eleven miles away. Charlie gives Cory lots of matrimonial advice, which Cory has enough good sense to ignore.

Carol and Charlie and the kids occupy the main ranch house. Its kitchen and two upstairs bedrooms were standing in 1903 when Charlie's grandfather arrived; succeeding generations have added a living room, a dining room, and two more bedrooms. Cory and Jennifer's bungalow started out life as a schoolhouse, Merrill lives in a double-wide trailer, and I stay in what was once a homesteader's cabin and later the cookhouse.

Calving on the Farthing ranch lasts about six weeks and is an all-consuming affair. The maternity wards take up several thousand acres. The largest ward, the Big Meadow, covers a couple of sections of good hay ground due east of the buildings. The Big Hill runs along one end and rises several hundred feet above the ranch. It is steep and extremely rocky, but cows like to go up there to calve. They can find green grass poking out from under rocks and cropping up sparsely in the clearings before stands of mountain mahogany. They can also find shelter from the interminable wind.

Farthings keep more cattle in a meadow referred to as Below-the-Lake and another hundred head in the Second Meadow, a smaller area west of the buildings. The Second Meadow is the most accessible area and here are the heifers (cows who haven't calved before), the heavies (cows who are about to calve), the big-teated cows, and anyone else who we think bears especially close watch. Patients in need of intensive care are brought back to the buildings, where there are three large corrals, a large yellow shed, a couple of smaller sheds, a Quonset hut, and a barn.

Each morning, after we feed and water the horses and whatever cattle we have in the sheds, Cory and Merrill take a pickup and a tractor and begin feeding cattle, Carol packs the kids into the Suburban and checks the meadows, and Charlie and I saddle up and ride the Big Hill.

April 4: A front came in today with high winds. Wind-chill, I heard on the news, reached 12 below. We've set up a warming booth with a space heater in the Quonset hut and brought three chilled calves in to use it. Heat is like magic to these little babies. An hour or two of warmth and they're so perky you'd never believe they'd been close to death. We pulled a backwards calf in the Second Meadow, and two more back at the buildings.

When we checked the Second Meadow after lunch, we found a black heifer down near the creek, ready to calve. We decided to check her again in another half hour and set to dehorning calves. We use a lye paste on the nubbins which causes less trauma than cutting the horns out at branding time. We catch the calves by hand rather than roping them—calves will often start squalling when they are roped and upset the whole herd, but we can sneak up on them on foot without raising so much Cain. When it's warm, the calves are lazy and sleepy and easy to catch; today, we didn't have much luck. We only pasted six or so. We checked back on the black heifer. Nothing had changed so we decided to get horses and bring her in.

As we headed back to the barn, Carol drove up. A heifer in the Big Meadow wouldn't mother her calf. Cory rode to the Big Meadow; Charlie and I went back for the black.

By the time we found her, her water bag was out. We trailed her in and put her in the chute. Charlie stripped out of his coveralls and rolled up his sleeve. He reached up inside her to see what the problem was but the more he felt around, the more puzzled he became. "Nobody's home in there," he said at last. What we thought was her water bag was really a thread of her afterbirth: she had already calved. Cory took her back to the creek; with luck, her calf is still alive and she will find it.

Our lives are organized entirely around the instincts and needs of cows. We are always watching. A cow standing away from the herd: watch her. She is thinking about calving. A cow with a kink in her tail: watch her. She may be about to shit or pee, but if she isn't, or if she does and the kink doesn't go away, she may be about to calve. If not, something else is wrong: she may not have lost all her afterbirth and needs to be cleaned. A cow lying down: watch her. She may be asleep but she may be about to give birth. You learn to read the subtle difference.

As school kids, Charlie and I visited the Denver Mint on a field trip. We looked down from a balcony at conveyor belts carrying thousands of pennies. Women stood over the belts and their hands moved in a blur as they picked out flawed coins. Their eyes had become accustomed to irregularity, and calving is something like that.

April 5: The black heifer who came up empty yesterday was still on the creek when we checked the Second Meadow this morning, so we figured we better start searching the creek banks. Charlie found her calf drowned, submerged in several feet of water. I couldn't see it at all but Charlie detected its little yellow hooves through the murkiness.

After we checked the Big Hill, Charlie sent me to the Second Meadow to bring in the black heifer so we could

*graft an orphan on her. By the time I arrived, the heifer
had left the creek for the hay ground. Several black heifers
were at feed and I didn't recognize her. I asked Cory if he
remembered any distinguishing marks. "Oh," he said, "she
has cropped ears, no ear tag, and some white on her bag."
How could I have missed all that?*

*About fifty calves a day are hitting the ground now,
and we're moving cattle around a good deal. I'm having
trouble keeping everyone straight. A couple days ago Charlie and I brought a heifer down from the Big Hill and at
lunch I realized I didn't remember much about her.
"What did she look like?" I asked Charlie. "Pretty much
a Hereford?"*

*"Well," he answered, "she's got a little red teardrop
below her left eye and a ring around her left ear. A green
ear tag. And the age brand on her hip, a zero, is almost
white."*

Imagine a maternity ward with eight hundred patients
who can't speak. Most don't wear identification bracelets
and they change rooms several times a day. Some mothers
get confused about which baby is theirs; others don't like
motherhood at all and simply wander off. The medical staff
has no time to keep records, but they have to remember
who's who.

The majority of cows calve just fine by themselves, but
on any given day a couple of dozen need attention. Heifers
have more trouble calving than older cows. On the other
hand, some older cows' teats get so large that their calves
can't suck and then we need to milk them by hand. Each

shed holds from three to ten critters, and each patient needs individualized care—the panda-faced cow won't let her calf suck, the all-red cow has a crippled calf that needs help in order to eat, the blue-roan calf is an orphan we need to graft, the brockle-faced calf needs medication. Everyone on the crew constantly brings new cattle in and turns others out. We have to keep each other informed and a precise vocabulary develops.

I've heard cows described as red, blue, yellow, orange, black, white, silver, grey, roan, and paint—but almost never brown. Not purple either (though I have heard purplish). A baldy is a black with a white face. And description hardly stops at color: panda-faced, snake-faced, pig-faced, girlish, devilish, sinister, grinning, smirking, red-eyed, wild-eyed, black-eyed, ring-eyed, pie-eyed, goggled, red-necked, ice-eared, eyebrowed, bob-tailed, black-hooved, dainty, staggy, porky, and sugar-frosted. As the number of cows and calves increases, so does the need for a specialized memory.

April 12: Had a prolapsed cow in the Second Meadow this afternoon. She wasn't too bad—the prolapse was about the size of a child's balloon sticking out beneath her tail, brilliantly red. We brought her in on horseback, put her in the chute in the yellow shed. Charlie asked me if I wanted to doctor her. Well, sure.

I asked if I should use a plastic sleeve. No, Charlie said, not for something as simple as this. I stripped out of my coveralls, rolled up my shirt sleeve. He told me to lift up the prolapse—to take it in my hand, being careful not to dig in my fingernails, and just lift it up. Usually, then, the cow would pee. This cow didn't. He told me to start pushing the prolapse back in. The cow started to strain. Just push gently, he said. In time, she'll let you in. The cow started to shit. Just keep pushing, Charlie said. I was making some progress. Then there was a point where everything just sort of sucked back into place. At that point, the cow started to pee. She peed and peed—she probably hadn't passed water since she prolapsed. Her relief was palpable. She started to eat the cottonseed cake from the trough in front of her. When she seemed settled, I pulled out. Charlie gave me some uterine boluses; I put them in, then we sewed her up: three big stitches, with packaging string, each one tied off distinctly. Very basic surgery, this. We poked her with penicillin and let her out of the chute. I had shit and blood and pee up to my armpit.

We reach a particular sort of intimacy with these cattle. I remember a detail from a novel I once read where a mother reached in and cleaned out her baby's compacted bowel with her fingers after other remedies had failed. The action was not grotesque; it was necessary, part of the unquestioned acceptance we come to with our own bodies and with those of our children and invalid parents. Our intimacy with these cows is no different. We come in each evening splattered with mud and milk and manure, stained with blood and amniotic fluid, stinking of afterbirth. It's hard to convey the sheer satisfaction of it all.

April 15: Found a starved calf on the Big Hill today. She was with her mother but too weak to suck. We carried her in, trailed the cow. Her mother doesn't have much milk so we bottle-fed her. She's so weak she may not make it.

Gusts measured 63 mph at the Air Force Base, and it seemed even windier here. Cory took the tractor and pulled the drag over the Bar Circle meadow; the broken-up manure came along in waves. The sandhill cranes are here now, and the wind catches them when they try to rise up from the creek banks. They look like gawky gliders, about to crash. At one point, I watched Charlie open a gate and his unbuttoned jacket flared out in the wind. He is so tall and thin and long-limbed, I almost expected to see him rise up like one of the cranes. Later, we spooked a couple of mallards when we rode along the creek; they beat their wings just as hard as they could trying to get back to the water, but the wind carried them in the opposite direction. The wind has been picking up small rocks, hurtling them with such force that they break the skin. I have scratches on my cheeks and around my left eye. The big plank corral gates are impossible to handle. I needed three tries to close the gate on the north side of the horse corral yesterday, and the wind was coming from the west.

At lunch, Chris said he wanted to come with us in the pickup to check the Big Meadow and Charlie told him to meet us in the Quonset hut in half an hour. But when we were ready to go, we couldn't find Chris. We knew he had come out from the house, but we couldn't find him anywhere. We called for him, but the wind took our words away. We finally found him: he had thought Charlie said behind *the Quonset and had been there all the time, out of sight and out of earshot. Charlie told Chris we'd been afraid that the wind had carried him away and that we'd find him splayed out on the barbed wire around the alfalfa, snagged like a tumbleweed.*

It's too windy to feed hay, so the bulls come running for cake. One big Charolais likes to eat out of my hand and I try to keep a couple pieces in my pocket for him. Today I forgot and he was much offended. He's a broadheaded bull, jowly and freckle-faced, affectionate. If I rub the soft spot on his forehead, he leans into my hand and rolls up his eyes. I've named him John Bell after my greatuncle, whom he resembles. When he bellers, he even sounds like Uncle John calling to Aunt Marie: "Mahhrhee!" Charlie is appalled that I would name a Charolais after a good Hereford man, but he has to admit the likeness.

I've come to think that the most frequently used phrase this time of year is "out of the wind." She's got a good place for him, out of the wind. I don't see how that little fellah can be so cold, he's out of the wind. Let's leave the pickup here, out of the wind. I'll just lay that hay here, out of the wind. The shed is noisy, but at least it's out of the wind.

Several years ago, Charlie and Merrill came out one windy morning during calving season and something didn't look right. As Charlie tells the story, it was like running into a friend who had just shaved off his mustache—you knew something was different but you didn't know what. Then they realized that the roof of the barn had disappeared. They scouted around and found it on the ground, in perfect shape, a hundred yards away. Another time, they came out from lunch to find that the pickup they had parked at the saddle shop had vanished. They figured they must have left it somewhere else and looked around. No pickup. They considered the possibility of theft, but no one could have driven into the ranch undetected. They searched for a couple of hours before they figured out that the wind had knocked it out of gear and pushed it into the lake.

People tolerate the wind, but no one ever gets used to it. Imagine conducting a day's business from the hood of a car traveling sixty miles an hour. Cory came to interview for his job here on a perfectly still day. He grew up in the sheltered mountains of Colorado, and Charlie warned him about the wind. The first day Cory worked, a breeze came up and he said, "I see what you mean." No, Charlie thought, you don't. Since then, Cory has come to understand what wind means in Wyoming and he's getting discouraged. Charlie keeps telling him that calm weather is ahead, but Cory doesn't quite believe it.

April 20: Last night, the wind died down. It often dies down at night for an hour or two but comes back up before morning. I've grown used to waking to the sound of it but this morning I woke at 5:00 and all I could think was: I don't hear the wind. I fell back asleep and then jerked awake to a vague white light. I thought it must still be early but I looked at my watch and saw it was 6:00. I put on my glasses and looked outside again: we had about five inches of snow.

Charlie and I didn't even do chores: we saddled up and headed for the Big Hill. Without the wind, the quiet was deafening. We could hear ducks mutter on the lake as we passed, and red-wing blackbirds chattered and twirped in the cottonwoods. We could hear our saddles squeak. We could hear the tractor feeding out hay down in the meadow. (At first, I couldn't figure out what it was. It sounded like the ocean.) Charlie and I caught each other talking in over-loud voices, as if we were speaking to deaf folk.

We expected to find all sorts of trouble up the hill, but we didn't have a single new calf. By the time we headed down, the temperature had warmed and the snow had started to melt. The ground was so hard, so completely sucked dry from the wind, that the snowmelt just stood on top of it.

Near evening, it started to snow again and we decided to bring in the heavies from the Second Meadow. The meadow was slick. Our horses slipped each time we turned and cows skated all over the place. A heifer made a break. Cory turned after it and his horse went down. Cory hit with a thump and somersaulted a couple times. He wasn't hurt but that's not to say he felt good. He broke some ribs in a snowmobile wreck a month ago and today, irrigating with Merrill, he picked up a rock and tore them loose again. The fall wasn't what you'd call therapeutic. But he

got away without the horse rolling on him, without any
new broken bones.

By the time we got everything in, we had about three
inches of snow on the ground. We fed and doctored our
other charges and finished up about 7:00. It wasn't a
terribly busy day, but it was a frustrating one. Cory's horse
went down, we lost a big Charolais cow and can't get her
calf to latch onto a wet nurse, lost one calf to cold and
may lose another to infection. We have around ten calves
in the various sheds right now, and each one needs help to
a greater or lesser degree.

On the other hand, the little starved calf has made an
amazing comeback. She's running around, bucking and
kicking and having a great time. Her mother's gone dry
and we're trying to find her a new one. In the meantime,
she'll snack off anybody. We've watched her sneak up to
other calves' mamas and steal a bite. They kick her off,
but anytime we have a cow in the chute, we let her have
a meal. Whenever one of us comes into the shed, she comes
over and rubs against us like a cat. She has a little brown
mark over her eyebrow and a silly grin on her face. We've
nicknamed her Hungry.

We are now three weeks into calving and all of us are
tired. There's never any time for rest. Anyone who isn't out
checking or bringing something in is back home taking care
of something else. Of course, we also have to keep up with
the usual work. It takes us three or four hours each morning
to feed everything in the several meadows, and there's nec-

essary maintenance: fix the fence where a heifer crashed through it, replace the fan belt on the Haymaster, change some irrigation dams to take advantage of the melting snow.

There's a rule to calving: just when you're busiest, you run into trouble. Now the temperature drops and the snow stays on the ground for a couple of days. For once, there is no wind. We'd been cursing it for days, but at least it broke up the snow. Without it, the glare is blinding, and a dozen cows sunburn their bags. Sunburn is as painful for a cow as for a human—sunburnt cows won't let their calves suck. We have to put them in the chute and milk them by hand. Range cows aren't used to being milked. It takes a lot of time and patience. Right now, calving seems endless.

April 24: Carol found a dead calf in the Big Meadow this morning, a big black-baldy that looked like it had been born healthy; probably the sack didn't break and it suffocated. The mother was a nice Hereford heifer, and Charlie and I rode out to get her so we could graft an orphan on her. We found her still with her calf, nosing it, licking it, trying to get it up. It would have been futile to try and herd her away from the calf so I put a rope around the calf's back leg and started to drag it toward home. The cow followed, humming and mooing, sniffing first one side of the calf and then trotting around to sniff the other, sure with each bump and jerk that her baby had come back to life. She followed me all the way to the buildings, over two miles. I led her right into the corral and shut the gate;

*then we took her calf and threw it in the back of the
pickup to take to the dead pile. She kept circling the corral,
looking for it.*

*We had a cow in the Second Meadow with bad mastitis
and her calf couldn't get enough to eat. We decided to
graft the calf onto the heifer. Charlie and I rode to the
Second Meadow and Carol followed in the Suburban. We
hog-tied the calf and loaded it in the car. Once the mastitis
cow realized we had kidnapped her baby, she was broken-
hearted. She ran after the Suburban, bellering all the
while. As Carol drove off, I noticed that the calf had
kicked off its piggin' string and was standing up in the
back of the car, peeing in Ryan's diaper bag.*

*Sunday night the temperature dropped to 5 degrees. We
lost two calves in the meadow but had three live ones born
on the hill. Carol found a particularly big newborn chilled
in the Big Meadow and brought it in for a dose of heat in
the warming booth. When it was warm, Charlie and I
took it back in the pickup. The back of the truck was filled
with fencing equipment so we put the calf in the cab with
us. It felt great by that time and was strong and hungry.
All it wanted to do was suck. It tried to suck my knee, my
wrist, the gear-shift knob, anything. A calf will butt its
mother's udder to make her let down her milk and this
calf kept butting reflexively. Each time it did, it bashed its
head against the dashboard. Charlie drove while I tried to
keep the calf from injuring itself. It was bawling all the
time, its voice deafening in the closed cab. The calf was so
healthy, so hungry, so warm and so strong—and here it*

was, in the cab of the pickup with us, knocking the truck
out of gear and causing the sort of ruckus that made me
want to continue doing this—exactly this—forever.

In this business of cattle raising, we exert our will. We
take a calf off a poor cow and graft it onto a good one. We
hobble a reticent cow until she lets her calf suck. We midwife these calves into existence, we care for them, sometimes
we even risk our lives for them, and they are ultimately
slated for slaughter. In this fact lies the essential irony of
our work. No one forgets that a live calf is money in the
bank. And yet a reverence remains. John Bell and Hungry
and the calf in the cab of the pickup are not merely units of
production; our connection to them is more than economic.
Day in and day out we confront the messiness of this business of living; if we live with slaughter, we also live with
nurture, with seasons and cycles, with birth and with death.

April 28: The weather has finally turned. Yesterday was
sunny and 50 degrees. This morning we woke to hoar frost
—all the tree branches, fence wires and grasses sparkled
in the sun. And there was lots of sun: it was a beautiful
cloudless, windless day.
Charlie and I spent the afternoon dehorning. I ran out
of paste so I held the horses while Charlie worked. It was
nice to laze and gawk awhile. A blackbird landed on an
Angus cow. She switched her tail and the bird hopped
further forward on her back. The cow switched again and
tossed back her head. This time she knocked the bird off.

It landed on the ground beside her; she turned and butted at it as if it were a dog.

Charlie grabbed a big red calf and it started bawling. A couple dozen mother cows came running. They formed a circle, each cow snorting and sniffing, stretching out her neck in an attempt to get close enough to smell the calf. As each one got a sniff and realized the calf wasn't hers, her ears drooped and she lost interest. One cow recognized her calf and moved right in, almost knocking Charlie over. He popped her on the nose with a glove and finished pasting the calf.

Carol drove over in the Suburban. Chris was in school but Tom and Ryan were with her. We watched a baldy have a calf up along the ditch. She laid down and gave birth in about a minute and a half. Then she got back up and started circling her calf, licking all the time, mooing to it softly, humming. Soon, she started licking it harder, as if she were trying to actually lift it with her tongue. It tried to get up a couple of times and didn't make it. Then it succeeded and stood on its wobbly new legs. "That's how you're 'sposed to do it," Tom observed. Sometimes the boys get bored riding around in the Suburban so much but today everyone was in a good mood.

The boys are learning, already and as if by osmosis, an ancient husbandry. Ranching for the Farthings is a family affair and has always been so. They recently took on a mortgage to buy several more sections of land, part of the old Hirsig Ranch on their border. Right now they don't need more acreage, but the chance to buy contiguous land is rare. If Chris and Tom and Ryan want to stay on the ranch and raise their own families, they will be able to do so. The debt is for the future, modest enough not to imperil the present.

The Farthing Ranch is the only long-time family ranch left in the Iron Mountain area and one of the few family ranches in the West with a secure future. Part of that security comes from the fact that the Farthings don't run on public grazing land, but a larger part comes from the fact that the ranch has always been managed with an eye to future generations. They have always been in debt, but not dangerously so. They have never been seduced by machinery or modernization. They are hardly backward—they have two big Haymaster tractors, for instance, and the sheds all have electricity and water—but the Farthings have weighed each purchase carefully and resisted extravagant expense. Their pickups are stripped-down vehicles without air-conditioning or FM radios; they still put up hay in loose stacks rather than in bales or loaves that require new and more sophisticated, single-use machinery. Already they are engaged in estate planning in order to assure that the boys can keep the ranch once Carol and Charlie are gone.

If the Farthings were to sell out, they would be wealthy indeed. As it is, they work seven days a week and enjoy a comfortable though modest material life—something comparable to what a reasonably successful small businessman or associate professor might enjoy. They have nice but unassuming homes and they can afford to take vacations—though they seldom do.

April 30: When Charlie and I get to the top of the Big Hill each day, we split and ride separate ridges. We seem to have developed a ritual with a pair of coyotes. As we ride west, they pass us—one on each ridge—going east. Sometimes they pass within fifty or sixty yards of our horses. We have a running conversation with them— "Well, Mr. Coyote, I didn't find any trouble back my way; how are things up ahead?" When the wind was so bad a couple of days ago, Charlie snuck up on his coyote. It was sniffing around a sagebrush and must not have heard him coming. Charlie got to within a few feet of it before it realized he was there. It jerked around and saw him, jumped straight up into the air and then took off. Since then, it has kept a greater distance in its morning rounds.

Pasted a lot of calves today, doctored the diphtheria steer, cleaned a couple of afterbirths, brought in a starved calf and its mother who has a sunburned bag. The ground is dry enough to start feeding cake again and John Bell is grateful. Mostly, we just took care of business. Nothing too strenuous, nothing too exciting. The weather makes everything easy.

It is nearly the end of April now, and calving season is winding down. New calves will trickle in for another couple of weeks, but the bulk of them are already on the ground.

I can read the past month in my hands. The back of my left one has two long, deep scratches from busting through the brush on Sadie Mae, in pursuit of a cow. Another cut runs the length of my thumb—a heifer kicked me when I was milking her out. On the palm is a blood blister from something I don't remember, and two deep holes from slivers that I picked up trying to remove the bars from the door to the cinder-block shed when I hurried to let in an angry cow. On my right hand, I have two more sliver holes, three blisters from dehorning paste, a burn from a pot, a cut from the bag-balm can, a rope burn across the lower pads of my fingers, and a variety of other miscellaneous nicks and scratches. My hands are sore—they hurt whenever I try to grip anything—and the kids have nicknamed me Scar Hand. I remember going through this every summer when I returned from school to work on the ranch. This is the point where my hands start getting tough. This time, they will just become useful and I will leave.

In my life in the city, I work long days. I break up the hours at my desk or in the classroom with long hikes in the woods near my home, with bicycling, with gardening. Physical activity keeps me grounded in my body; time outdoors keeps me aware of the seasons. And yet here, in the country, is the real work, the interweave of man and animal, weather and land, that is as old as appetite. Here, physical exertion matters. It keeps me aware of what it means to be alive, and what it costs.

Bones

My father on Tequila

At Laguna, when someone dies, you don't "get over it" by forgetting; you "get over it" by remembering.

— *Leslie Marmon Silko*

It is hot August, high noon under an airless sky, and my father and a hired hand have brought in a sick bull for doctoring. I am four years old, maybe five, and I sit on a corral rail to watch. I smell horse sweat and the black, watery manure that the bull swipes with his tail in an arc across his ass. Dust cakes in my nostrils and around the edges of my mouth. I want to go back to the coolness of the house, but I also want to watch. I rub my mouth with the back of my hand and stay.

The bull is on the fight and he paws the ground. His eyes are dull and green with sickness, and when he throws his head and bellers, long strands of snot stream from his mouth and fly back across his shoulders, raising a few of the flies that blanket his rump.

When my father rides into the corral, the bull tries to take him. My father pivots his horse out of the way and ropes the bull, pulls him up short to the snubbing post and dallies around. He passes the end of the rope to the hired man, who has come into the corral on foot. Once the bull is secure, my father dismounts, ties his horse to a fence post, and returns with boluses and a syringe full of antibiotic.

The bull grumbles, fights the rope, snorts. But he is sick and he grows calmer with fatigue. My father jabs the needle into the animal's thigh. The bull rears back against the rope. The wraps on the post slip. The bull breaks loose, snot flying in an arc, his beller blue and loud.

From the fence I watch as he takes my daddy down. The world erupts in dust and blood. The bull is roaring, groaning, grinding, someone is yelling, my father is a tiny spider of flailing arms and legs.

I hear the hired hand crying over and over, "Oh my God, oh my God, oh my God." He tries to snub the bull again but he might as well attempt to drag a mountain from its plain. Finally, he gains a wrap of rope and my father rolls free. I watch as he crawls across the corral, climbs the fence hand over hand, his heavy legs dangling uselessly beneath him. He casts himself over the top rail, crashes in a grunt of dust on the other side. The bull bellers and falls silent. The dust settles. Everything is perfectly still.

My father was loaded onto a door and taken to town in the back of a pickup. A few weeks later he came back, and though he walked with a limp, he took up his regular chores. The bull, too, recovered. He was a quality bull and we kept him until he was too old to service cows. Then we shipped him to the packers.

We. A few weeks ago, I learned that this happened before I was born. I have carried it like a memory, but it's not a memory; it's a story I've heard, fleshed out by details told down through the years. I'm amazed. I cannot imagine this event without also imagining myself within it, watching. ·

Few occupations are as physically threatening as arid-country cattle ranching. Professional football is; roughnecking on an oil rig; logging. And like other occupations that depend on the body yet place it constantly in peril, cattle ranching breeds an attitude toward danger of both reverence and disdain.

Our neighbor Buddy Hirsig always helped us brand. One time his horse fell on him and broke his ankle as we brought cattle into the corral. "Do you mind if I rope today?" he asked my father. "I can't walk so good and I'd rather stay horseback."

"Oh hell," my father answered. "We have plenty of help. Go on home." But Buddy insisted on staying, and no one was surprised. He roped calf after calf with unerring accuracy and only when the day's work was finished did he cut off his boot and head to town to get his ankle casted.

I remember a term: major plaster. Minor injuries—a broken wrist, a sprained ankle, a cut requiring stitches— were too insignificant to mention. Major plaster meant serious injury, something that would take months, even years, to heal. A cast on an arm didn't count. One from toe to ass did. So did body casts or almost anything requiring traction. Community gatherings nearly always found someone in major plaster, and Iron Mountain was not a large community. If everyone came together at the same time, including visiting aunts and the Chesers' basset hound, they might have numbered sixty.

Each new badge of plaster met with predictable banter. "You *needed* a vacation." "That's one way to get sympathy." "It's about time you broke something. The doc's youngest son just graduated high school." (Dr. Klein was the bone doctor in Cheyenne and we were convinced our debilities paid for his children's Ivy League educations.)

The quips and wisecracks were a lie, a safe way to say "I'm sorry." Injury meant doctors' bills—huge doctors' bills —often in a time of high interest rates, low cattle prices, and drought. Injury meant one less person to do the work. Injury meant more strain on the marriage. Injury meant new insult to a body already prematurely old. And injury meant pain, acute pain for a while and then chronic pain that flared each time the barometer fell. But injury also promised resurrection. If you were injured, at least you weren't dead.

Another memory. I am eight years old and wearing a lime-green tutu when Harold, our foreman, comes through the door from the thunderstorm outside to tell my mother that Dad has broken his leg. His horse slipped on a bridge. I am to be in a ballet recital that night in town. "What about me?" I ask.

"We'll try to make it on time," she says.

A hired hand's smashed thumb a few days before has wiped us out of codeine, so she gives my father aspirin before they load him on the door. This time they put him in the back of our station wagon. During the two-hour ride through mud and rain to town, he calls me his ballerina cowgirl and recites Kipling to pass the time:

> *Yes, Din! Din! Din!*
> *You Lazarushian-leather Gunga Din!*
> *Though I've belted you and flayed you,*
> *By the living Gawd that made you,*
> *You're a better man than I am, Gunga Din!*

I danced that night, though my father didn't see me. Both bones in his lower leg had been crushed and four hours of surgery left him with a three-inch pin in his calf. The bones had been broken so many times before, they wouldn't knit. He wore a hip cast for a year and a half, and a brace for another year. With the cast, he couldn't ride, he couldn't drive, and he couldn't climb our narrow stairway, so he slept on the Hide-A-Bed in the living room.

He could weld and he worked long hours in the shop, the plastered leg stretched out in front of him. We accused him of welding every piece of metal on the ranch together, and in fact he soon ran out of work. He bought a Heathkit and built an FM radio. Diagrams, tiny wires, and transistors were scattered across the dining-room table for weeks and he soldered patiently. When he finished, the radio worked fine, but we were too far out in the country to pick up any signals.

Once the cast came off, he bought a therapeutic boot to which weights could be attached. Each night he sat in his shorts on the island in the kitchen and strapped it on. He'd straighten the leg again and again until his T-shirt was soaked with sweat. I remember the grind of his teeth as he worked at the weights, and the way tears squeezed out of the corners of his eyes.

You did what you had to and went on. Accommodation, not much talked about, was key. People in Iron Mountain still talk of Mrs. Steele, who ran a nearby ranch by herself after her husband went crazy. A horse fell on her and broke her arm. The arm never bent right after that, and she had trouble combing her hair, so she wore it cropped short, like a man's.

A cowhand's walk, shaped by years of damage and recovery, is a study in accommodation. The body cants forward from the waist, the lower back fuses, the hips stiffen, the walk becomes awkward, the head seems to settle into the shoulders. "It's a kink in the neck," one old-timer told me, trying to describe his own gait, "and a limp in every limb."

Not all accommodation is physical. One night, when my father was rehabilitating his leg and had finished eighty repetitions with fifty pounds, he joked to my mother, "See that? It's almost good enough to break again." Through two and a half years, she had been calm, caring, full of humor. She had chauffeured him to the fields each morning and waited until frustration made him ask to go back home. She had arranged her work in the house around his presence. She had made up his bed on the sofa. She had carted the things he couldn't carry, accomplished the chores he couldn't do. All this without complaint. But that night she turned to him. "Larry," she said without a smile, "break it again and I'll treat you like a horse."

The psychology of accommodation is letting things go. "Sooner or later," one woman told me, "the other boot is going to drop. No sense worryin' until you hear the crash." Then, she might have added, you pick up the pieces. Buddy Hirsig bought a dirt bike to use around the ranch. The first time he chased a cow, the bike hit a rock and he catapulted over the top. He was traveling fifteen or twenty miles an hour when he lit on his hands. They swelled up like hams. He couldn't hold a fork, turn a doorknob, work a button. Glenna, his wife, didn't mind dressing him or feeding him or even attending to his personal needs. What she minded, she said, was helping him smoke. The ability to mine calamity for punch lines may be the most important accommodation of all.

It never occurred to me that the men and women I grew up with were courageous. Israeli writer and war correspondent Yaël Dayan, the daughter of General Moshe Dayan, once wrote that her father could not be called courageous because he had no fears to overcome. As a child, it seemed to me that my people were similarly fearless, and being fearless, they were invulnerable. I was not alone in this illusion. Carol Horn, a rancher in North Park, Colorado, told me about watching her grandmother thrown off a hay rake by a runaway team. "Here she was," Carol recalled, "in her sixties, being rolled around under the rake. I wasn't even concerned about it, because it was Grandma. Grandma took care of everything. She had that much control."

In this world of bashed and battered bodies, I felt safe. Injury was real, but it didn't seem to matter much. The injured could rise, phoenixlike, from the ashes of catastrophe, and their feats of recuperation still amaze me. When a horse fell on my seventy-two-year-old Great-aunt Marie and broke her pelvis in three places, the doctors told her she would never ride again. Two months later, she proved them wrong. Merrill Farthing was in his eighties when he fell on a fence spike and punctured his lung. When he finally agreed to go to town, he had double pneumonia and the doctors advised the family to hover near. Three weeks later, Merrill left the hospital and soon returned to the fence line.

With such models around me, I wanted my chance. By the time I entered fourth grade, I had started cutting deals with God. Each night before I went to sleep, I would pray, "Please, God, let me break my leg tomorrow." I dreamed of the kids at school scribbling their names on my cast, but more than that, I wanted the badge of plaster, the proof that the horses I rode were as tough as those of the men, that I wasn't afraid, that I could "take it."

But I didn't break my leg. So I upped the ante. "Please,

God. If you'll break my leg tomorrow, I'll be nice to my brother for a *whole year*." And then, when my limbs remained discouragingly sound, "Please, God, break my leg tomorrow or I won't believe in you anymore." And finally, "Okay, okay, I'll settle for a broken arm. Are you up there, God? Are you listening?"

I thought my people were immortal. Deep down, I had always understood that ranch accidents could be tragic. I knew that Biddy Bonham's father had been killed when his horse tripped in a gopher hole, and that old Mr. Shaffer died when he fell off a haystack. But these deaths were so distant from me they hardly seemed real. Then, when tragedy struck close to home, it had nothing to do with the roughness of our work. "The danger," my mother used to say, "is never where you think it is." Which was her way of saying "Look behind."

The night my mother died of an aneurysm at the University Hospital in Denver, my father, brother, and I returned to the Brown Palace Hotel. It was ten o'clock at night, maybe midnight, and we called room service. I ordered vichyssoise, my favorite Brown Palace dish since childhood, and when it came, I took the silver covering off the china bowl. I sprinkled the soup with lime, as I always did, and I remember gazing at the perfect little drops of juice, floating on the surface like tiny shimmering planets. I couldn't get any further and my father, too, pushed his dinner away.

" 'If you can make one heap of all your winnings,' " he

said at last, quoting Kipling who always seemed to come to him in crisis,

> *And risk it on one turn of pitch and toss*
> *And lose and start again at your beginnings*
> *And never breathe a word about your loss . . .*

And then he put his face in his hands and broke down. I remember the hugeness of him hunched in his chair. I remember a single tear breaking through the dam of his fingers, winding its way down his broad weathered cheek to catch in his quivering mustache.

In the wide-open spaces of ranch country animal remains are common. When you work with a young colt, there comes a day when you take him up to the bones. A colt will spook at them, even when the bones are decades old. Unless you work to overcome that fear, the colt will always shy away. There will be places in the world the colt can't walk. But if you take time, urge the colt closer and closer, not denying its fear but not turning away from it either, the horse will eventually approach what scares him. He will see that bones are just bones. He will move in the world more freely.

Ranchers walk up to most bones. They look physical danger right in the eye and don't blink. But there are other bones that scare them. For my family, the pile we shied away from was grief. Everything in my background prepared me to deal with physical pain. Nothing prepared me for emotional loss.

When my father worked his repetitions with the leg weight, he let the tears flow freely because he knew, when the session was over, he could turn to us with a wry smile. But he never again shared his grief with us after we left that hotel room. We went through the automatic motions of a funeral, returned to the ranch, and sorted through my mother's belongings. Within days, we had discarded almost everything that might remind us of her.

Long before the pain had started to abate, we declared it over. "It's time," my father said, "to rejoin the human race." I returned to college. My father met and soon married a woman who looked exactly like my mother. The marriage was painful for both partners and ended in divorce. And for years I spent so much energy denying my own longing for the dead that I hardly had energy for the living.

If any of us had broken a leg, we would have taken all the time the leg required. If the bone didn't knit in six months, we would have given it twelve. And if it still wasn't sound, we would have strapped on a brace. We might have asked each other, "How's that leg?" But we didn't ask, "How's that loneliness?" We tried to put our grief behind us, but we had only shied away from it. We started walking before we had healed. For years we hardly mentioned my mother's name. And we soon found there were places we didn't dare walk.

I remember nothing of my mother's funeral, absolutely nothing, until the end when we were leaving the cemetery.

A neighbor, Sandy Hirsig, Glenna and Buddy's daughter, came up to me. She was a few years my junior, but I had always felt a particular connection with her—she, too, was close to her mother. She approached me just as I was about to get into the limousine, and she hugged me. I had this curious sense of looking down on the two of us as if from above and thinking: She is the only one who could possibly understand.

And then, when just a few years later Sandy was killed in a brutal accident on the Iron Mountain road, I couldn't sleep for nights. She and her mother had been driving to the ranch, and I could almost hear the intense conversation before they came around a corner and slammed into a snowplow; my mother and I always had our very best conversations on that fifty-mile stretch of road. I wrote the Hirsigs the polite, formal letter of sympathy I had been trained to write, and I never told even the man I was living with about the accident, though he was a sensitive man. I was too afraid that, in the telling, I wouldn't take it well— I would break down.

A few months later, I returned to Wyoming and visited the Hirsigs. I wanted to tell them what I hadn't been able to mention in the letter—how Sandy came up to me at my mother's funeral and gave me the single moment of true solace that penetrated that horrible affair. But I couldn't tell them. We talked for an hour and I never mentioned Sandy's name. Buddy Hirsig had ridden all day with a broken ankle at our branding, but I was afraid to tell either him or Glenna how much their daughter touched me. I was too afraid of making them sad, of challenging their ability to take it, of challenging mine.

And losses piled upon losses. Other members of my family passed away, I lost friends to accidents and cancer. I kept reinforcing the dam with each new addition. I left my lover and since I had no place to put my sadness, I started watching movies. I saw *The Black Stallion* eleven times. A boy and a stallion are the sole survivors of a shipwreck and they make it to a desert island. The first half of the film is done almost entirely without dialogue. Halfway through, the boy and the horse are discovered and returned to civilization and then the story becomes just another film. But the first half: something about such deep and wordless communication in total isolation touched me. Eleven times I bought a ticket. Eleven times I sat alone in the dark and wept from the moment the horse first appeared on the screen until the midway point. And then I'd dry my eyes, pick up my bag, and leave.

At some point, I sought out a therapist. I don't remember the year, I don't remember the particulars of despair. There is so much about those years I don't remember. It was the hardest decision I had ever made, an admission, if only to myself, that I couldn't take it. In the first session, I started to cry. I couldn't stop. I remember the terror—my God, I will never stop. I wept in session and I wept out of session. I hid myself away so friends wouldn't know. They didn't miss me; I had already been absent for a long time.

Tears, like rain, can't last forever. In time the flood receded, and I had a sense of emerging into a world that seemed just born: the air crisp, the rustle of leaves surprising and new.

When you take a colt near the bones, every muscle in his body is posed in opposition. He may, at your urging, nudge forward, but his energy is entirely consumed by the posture of escape. If fear overcomes him, he will bolt blindly, crashing into a fence or stumbling over a bank. But if he inches up to the bones, bit by bit and soft assurance by assurance, he will smell them, his ears will twitch a time or two and then fall back in bored relaxation. At that point his whole body will relax, visibly and at once, and in a moment he will be focused on the outside world again, anxious to get on with the rest of the journey.

In eighteen years of intermittent ranch work, I never had a serious injury: no major plaster. Recently, though, I had a physical and I was asked to fill out a health questionnaire. When I met with the doctor, she started asking about my relationships with men. I answered the first couple of questions perfunctorily, but after the third, I asked her why she cared. "Seven brain concussions," she read off my list of injuries. "A broken cheekbone, a broken rib, bruised kidneys..."

How often, I thought later, she must read physical scars for the emotional ruin they hide. How often her questions must probe the deepest shame. But as I explained my own history, I recognized a hint of pride in my voice. I had paid my dues in the world of work. I could "take it." Sometimes, now, physical endurance seems the easy part, but it holds lessons for me if I will only listen.

Almost every ranch-stead is littered with bones. The skull of a bull, a deer, or an antelope tacked up over a gate or barn door, a pile of elk antlers by the shed, a cow pelvis in the garden. When you find a bone—a buffalo skull, a bobcat jaw, the precise, tiny foot of a badger—you bring it home. The larger piles you leave alone. Skeletons mark the method of dying, at least until time and coyotes rearrange the evidence. A small pelvis hung up in a larger one: breech birth. Backbone downhill, head flung upward gasping for one last breath: poison weed.

Even to my house in the city, I drag home bones: a deer head for the hearth, a bull skull for the entryway. There's a stark beauty to bones, bleached white by the sun. Bones are as hard as rock and as fragile as rock. They crack, fissure, shatter, and as they wear to dust, they take us with them, both column and conduit of our own evolution. In the bloodline drawn by landscape, all bones are ancestral. Our homage is sincere and yet irreverent, a wry celebration of the fact that we still wrap our own bones with skin.

Marie

My Great-aunt Marie and John, shortly after their marriage

In my Great-aunt Marie's vision of heaven, all the horses and all the dogs she had ever loved would come running to meet her when she came through the gate. The people she cared for—her husband John, her friends Tom and Irene, Isabel and Beanie and Floyd—would be there, too, but quieter and more in the background, at least until she had satisfied herself that her critters were happy and well-fed.

This is how I remember Marie: a slender woman of medium height who often wore blue and who had the purest white hair imaginable, pulled back in a French twist, and amazingly tidy, even in a branding corral on a hundred-degree day. She was constantly in motion and in her later years she trotted everywhere, as if she didn't have enough time left to fit everything in. I think of her always reaching out to something—to chuck the ear of her good dog Spike, to slip a piece of cake to her Sweetheart mare, to pull an orphan calf's head to the nipple on the milk bucket, to hand a drink to a friend or sprinkle a little flour in the gravy. She had large sky-blue eyes that glowed, even near the end when they had a milky, almost shattered look about them. I wanted to grow up to be just like her, and once, when I was a child, I spent a whole afternoon and a summer's wages at a carnival booth in order to win a large stuffed cat that reminded me of Marie—bright blue with jeweled blue eyes, round cheeks, and a look of delighted contentment.

It was the contentment I remember most. In her later years Marie was visited with sorrow, as the old so often are, for what she had loved and lost, but even the sorrow was woven into a sense of harmony, an unavoidable component in a life tied to land and animals and seasons. I believe I have never met another person so entirely at ease with her life. I was Marie's only close female blood relative and I always felt the privilege of it. I loved to be touched by her calm. And yet Marie revealed little of her inner self. She was a presence in the world, but you never knew what she was thinking.

After Marie died in 1984, I inherited her diaries. Floyd Hale, her foreman of over fifty years and one of her closest friends, gave them to me. "Marie told me to destroy these," Floyd said, "but I think you should have them. I think Marie would want you to have them."

Floyd was a stocky man, given to few words. The bulk of his power was in his torso, and I remember the way he held the small books in his thick hands, and the gravity with which he handed them over. I took them with a sense of responsibility and awe and, though I poked around in them from time to time, I didn't sit down to really read them for some years. The penmanship was an excuse: Marie had a large, cursive hand that was almost illegible when cramped onto the narrow lines. But that wasn't really the reason. I was afraid, I suppose, that the Marie I would find in their pages would be at odds with the Marie I loved.

But the diaries had their own quiet insistence about them, not unlike Marie. There came a time I couldn't stay away and I set to reading them, gradually learning to decipher the loops and swirls and overwrites. They were daybooks, mostly in pocket-sized, five-year diaries, for nineteen of the twenty-eight years from 1936 through 1963. In them I found a woman who was just like the Marie I thought I knew.

MAR 21, 1938: While in Denver John heard Talbott place for sale. . . .

By the time Marie and John learned that the Graham-Talbott Ranch at Iron Mountain was for sale, they had been married for sixteen years. They ran the Bell Packing Plant in Cheyenne and leased a ranch called the Polo. John was away at least half the time, buying cattle, trading horses, heading down to Mexico to contract longhorn steers for the Cheyenne rodeo. The day-to-day management of the plant fell to Marie, and she must have hated the closeness of it, the smell, the daily routine: unloading cattle from railroad cars, sending them through the killing room and the skinning line, hanging the carcasses on big metal hooks, pushing them into the dark coolers where they would gently sway. It was the middle of the Great Depression; the middle, too, of a desperate and prolonged drought. "It was terrible," she told me, "just terrible. There was no grass anywhere, nothing for cattle to eat. You couldn't sell them—there was no market. The government started a relief program, buying cattle for a few dollars a head. Some were too weak to ship; they just killed them where they were. Others, they sent to us. We'd open a carload and they'd be glassy-eyed, so starved they'd eaten each other's ears and tails off. You never want to see it, I'll tell you."

What Marie wanted, what she had always wanted, was a ranch of her own: clean air, spaciousness, feed for her animals, security. Land prices plummeted; Marie and John started looking for a ranch they could afford. The Talbott place, just a few miles from where Marie had been raised, was a dream come true.

MAR 22, 1938: Not much news. John & I talking & figuring ranch most of time

MAR 29, 1938: I hope I hope

MAR 30, 1938: Almost decided to go ahead with ranch. . . . Things will work out.

Mar 31, 1938: Guess I never was so glad. A big
day in our lives   signed contract for Talbott &
Graham ranch $32,000.00   believe it is a good
investment   ranch in good shape   lots of hay
left

In May, they started moving their cattle from the Polo
out to Iron Mountain. The cattle were weak: "... was hard
on cattle moving them   bummed some calves & lost several cows." In addition, the poison weed—larkspur—was
in bloom, tauntingly delicious when there was so little grass:
"Lost 3 good cows with poison weed.... had over 20 down
at one time.... I took shots out to them."

But they got the cattle to the ranch and then the work
started in earnest: "lots to do sure." They tried to give up
their lease on the Polo, but the owners wanted them to stay
until the ranch could be sold. They divided their time between the two places, and each time Marie had to leave her
own ranch, she was sad: "John & I leaving for Polo.... I
didn't dare look back   we don't like girls that cry."
Homesickness haunted her whenever she was away:
"Would like to be back in our little home on our own
place. Life is like that." Every time she headed home, she
celebrated: "Going home today   guess I am awfully
silly but love it there." On December 31, she wrote, "The
last day of 1938   beautiful day. this was one of the grand-
est years I have ever had   got ranch   made all our
payments   very happy."

She cooked for John and "her boys," Floyd and Herb

and Red and whoever else was on the payroll, doctored them when they were sick, ironed, cleaned, maintained the bunkhouse and the cookhouse, worked inside the house, worked outside with cattle. And she and John quickly settled into the neighborhood. Beanie and Isabel Hirsig, Grayce and Merrill Farthing, Tom (Merrill's brother) and Irene Farthing who ran the store, Marie's brother Sunny— everyone was young and healthy and filled with the devil. They helped each other out and then danced until dawn. There was a sort of seamless quality to the life depicted in the daybooks, with little line between work and play:

SEPT 7, 1938: John & Sam left for Lusk to buy cattle. I . . . went to B Hirsigs with Tom & Irene. John came later more fun   home at 3 A.M.

OCT 29, 1938: Shipped out Mr. Graham's cows & calves. Went to Merrill Farthing's for dinner then to Tom's for school program and dance & did we have fun. . . . about the best time I ever had.

NOV 16, 1938: Floyd put another coat of plaster on kitchen   wind blowing 87 miles   I fixed chicken with dressing & noodles   the boys were certainly tickled   John home 5 P.M. Bridge club at Toms (fun)

It was a pattern that never really changed through the years, and the sheer amount of work recorded in the daily entries is mind-boggling, as during March of 1944 when

Marie painted the bathroom and both bedrooms, including closets and bedroom furniture; cleaned up and painted the cookhouse; remodeled Floyd's bunkhouse room; and helped with the calving during a particularly blizzard-ridden March. Work sustained Marie, and she reported it with a cheery pride. She sometimes admitted fatigue, but never once in all the years did she complain about the work itself: "John & I worked cattle this A.M.   windy & cold   took cattle out of School Sec in P.M.   put them on top   a little tired but love it."

And always, intertwined with the work, was the sense of community:

FEB 21, 1944: Monday. Sprayed 1050 cattle here [for lice]. Short about 18 head. Della & Grayce helped me & fed 15. Through about 4:30. Beautiful day.

FEB 22, 1944: sprayed 1200 at B Hirsigs. I went over & helped Isabell. Very windy. Lots of fun.

FEB 23, 1944: Wednesday. Sprayed about 1200 at Merrills. I helped Grayce. Bridge club at our house in evening. Everyone tired.

Or this entry, from 1958:

More ironing then I went to Wilma's and cut her hair   it looked good   came home and cut Mary's and it looks nice too. Grayce & Wilma came up in the afternoon and I cut hers. had fun all day

John and Marie couldn't have children, but they took in friends and particularly longtime help as family. Floyd had joined John and Marie before they bought the Iron Mountain ranch, managing a feed operation in Nebraska. When they bought the Graham-Talbott Ranch, Floyd moved to Iron Mountain. He was an intimate friend, more like a brother than an employee or even a manager. Where the other hired men lived in the bunkhouse, Floyd had his own, separate living quarters. He ate most of his meals with John and Marie, even when a ranch cook fed the other men. The three of them often talked long into the night and they went everywhere together.

MAY 27, 1939: Snow all day but they finished shipping 1607 sheep about 3 P.M.   everyone a little tired   John Floyd & I had big rummy game

FEBRUARY 28, 1942: John Floyd & I rode all A.M. took colts back to Greecewood   went to see stud & cows & calves. [The three of us] went to Plains Hotel dance . . . had so much fun . . . got home about 3:00 A.M.

FEB 22, 1947: Getting things ready for Floyd's party we set up tables & got dishes ready & silver out going to have Fr[esh] Lobster dinner, Shrimp etc baked 2 cakes   1 chocolate 1 Sponge   good

Floyd stayed as Marie's foreman after John's death in 1972. As her health and eyesight failed, Floyd chauffeured her around, looked after her, even cooked for her. More than any other person, he made it possible for her to remain at Iron Mountain. Floyd was only a few years younger than Marie, and his life, like hers, had been devoted to the ranch. Almost exactly a year after her death, he died. He is buried next to John and Marie.

Other longtime help became family. There was Mary, the kindhearted, wall-eyed cook who worked for the ranch in the 1950s and 1960s, and Elwood and Myra Hannah, who were with John and Marie during the same period. And then there was Melvin Wright. Mel came to John and Marie for his first job fresh out of high school in 1955, and he had won a place in their hearts by the time he was called into the service in 1958:

APRIL 7, 1958: Melvin . . . takes his physical in Denver tomorrow   Sure hate to see him go But know he will have to

Nov 1, 1958: Wilma & Jim, John & I had party for Melvin   had his folks and there was 22 of us they seemed to have a good time. hate to see Melvin go and will be glad when he gets home

DEC 15, 1958: Mel is coming home for Xmas and I am glad

DEC 28, 1958: Sunday. Beautiful day. Mel came up and spent the day with us and we sure did enjoy visiting with him   Gave him his bonus check for $250.00   He is a good boy   hope he comes back to us   He has to leave Jan 3 for camp

APRIL 25, 1959: John and I are going to the
Kentucky Derby   Mel will go with us from Ft.
Knox

John and Marie kept in touch with Mel during the time
he was in the Army, and kept his job open for him on his
return:

OCT 14, 1960: This is a good day   Melvin leaves
Germany for U.S.   should be here again by Nov 1
we'll all be glad to see him. Hope he is us.

Nov 6, 1960: Sunday   Beautiful day   did a
little cleaning and the usual things. John & Bill went
over to Pascoe   Floyd & Melvin to Wheatland. . . .
Sure seems good to have Melvin home again. Don't
know how we got along without him.

When Mel fell in love, he brought his bride back to the
ranch:

DEC 24, 1961: Melvin Wright and Daisy Graham
were married   Mary & I went to the wedding
Mary stayed in Wheatland and I came home   and
we had such a nice Xmas Eve

JAN 3, 1962: Melvin & Daisy are back from their
honeymoon & they are settled. . . . think we are so
lucky in our good help.

John and Marie attributed much of their success to the work of their "good help." In the 1960s, they set up the Iron Mountain Ranch Company to include Floyd and the Wrights in ownership and profit sharing. John and Marie left the Peaden Ranch to the Wrights and land and a life estate at Iron Mountain to Floyd. They also provided for the Hannahs and Mary.

Marie's sense of family was not limited to people. The longest entries in the daybooks are the obituaries she wrote for her favorite animals:

MARCH 25, 1937 —Joe died   he was 28 years old   John broke him at the Happy Jack Ranch. . . . 24 years ago   was a fine old horse   blaze faced bay   he adopted a little black colt when its mother died and watched over it till it was a yearling they were great cronies and he felt he was doing something worthwhile and they still call horses dumb animals. He was up in the upper meadow and managed to get home to die   he did love it here in his old Barn & yard.

MARCH 3, 1938: Red found King up in sand draw poor old fellow couldn't get up and Red had to kill him   My old horses are almost all gone now and I know they are all in a swell place where there are lots of green grass and oats. May we all meet and have some good rides again.

APRIL 24, 1938: Mrs. Tye called said one of our horses was down   it was Popcorn   had broken

leg. Red had to shoot him. . . . what a horse   he
was to England three times as Rope horse   he
loved it and did so want to do his part   I fed him
Oats many a day to keep him alive the past couple
years. and he is with his old pals Slim & King
Boys going to bury him. so farewell to a fine horse
and such a loyal friend.

Marie mentioned her critters as often in her daily ac-
counts as she did the people in her life, and their lives were
intimately wound up with her own.

SEPT 9, 1944: Saturday. Busy all day cooking &
cleaning but the dogs [Mike and Patsy] stayed home
& helped me. Don't know how I would live without
Mike.

SEPT 13, 1944: Wed. Nice day in Denver. I looked
around in the stores John & Floyd to yards & C & S.
got some vegetables. Mikey so glad to see us home. (I
love that dog so much.)

SEPT 14, 1944: Thursday. busy day. I put up pears.
Grayce & Merrill up in evening. Jack & Della up too.
Mike sure did show off & entertain everyone tonight.

SEPT 16, 1944: A party at Davis ranch. My Mike
was killed. Cowboy [probably another dog] grabbed
him in front of Floyd's car & it killed him. Look in
back of this book. I loved Mike more than anything
I had.

In the back of the diary, under "Memoranda," Marie had written, "Mike my boy your work is all done and you did it well" and then penned this remembrance:

SEPT 16, 1944—MIKE

This day ended the life of my little dog Mike. He was borne Feb 26—1937. I loved him more every day he lived. I believe he was the sweetest dog I ever saw. He helped us put up hay. He didn't quite get it done. I guess that is true with all of us we never quite get it all done. He tried so hard and I know when I go he will come running to meet me as he always did and he will be just waiting for me for he was my dog and he knew no other dog would ever take his place. Good boy Mike. I won't have to tell you to be a good dog this time. And some of these days I will be seeing you. God bless you and keep you for me. Your pardner.

Marie struggled, over the next few weeks, to accommodate to the loss of her little friend:

SEPT 17, 1944. Sunday. A very sad day at our house. We buried my Mike just back of the yellow Rose bush under the cottonwood. Floyd made him a nice casket. God take care of him for me.

SEPT 19, 1944: Put up 25 pints of Chile sauce. John Floyd & Buck to Pascoe to fix windmills. Smithy

back. I was so lonesome for my little pardner   I
just must get used to it I guess   I will try.

Sept 30, 1944: Saturday. Two weeks ago my Mike
was killed . . . enough said. Busy all day

Oct 2, 1944: Rained nearly all day. Hope it lasts a
week. Did a big washing & boy is it wet. Floyd made
Mike's tomb stone and I wrote his name & dates on it.

Mike stayed in her thoughts. Two years later:

Sept 16, 1946: Mon. Floyd Jim & I gathered cattle
up on top   brought them down to Hay Canyon
lots of trouble   Mike dead two years today

Marie loved all animals. She loved the cows she cared
for daily, she loved the deer that grazed in the meadow and
often came up onto her lawn. Eating meat, both domestic
and wild, was a part of the natural order of which she was
a part, an ancient trade of sustenance for care. She helped
butcher the crippled heifer; she got out the canning equipment when the boys brought in a deer. But she hated the
annual pogrom known as hunting season.

Oct 9, 1947: Thurs. Deer season opened today
they are slaughtering them & I love them so. I guess
I can't stop them. They are taking them out in car
loads

OCT 11, 1947: Sat. Hunting all day & all night
God how I hate them

One of the few times Marie recorded a spat with John
had to do with animals:

JAN 9, 1962: John sold all our old horses   why
wouldn't he let them be put away by a vet and let
them be home to die   why is money so necessary
I shed many tears over this   hope I don't have to
see this again

Marie would have described herself as a simple person
and in this way she was: She had a single desire, a single
focus—the ranch was all she wanted.

John and Marie made a colorful pair. Marie, so slim and
tidy, seemed always forward on her toes. John was a great
big slack-jawed fellow with a booming voice who somehow
made everyone feel at ease. The two of them had a sense of
both appetite and generosity, and when you were around
them you couldn't help feeling that the world was a splendid place.

When John was away, he wrote Marie often, sometimes
twice a day. When he returned, he always brought her
something—"the cutest little radio for the kitchen," or "the
most beautiful bag." Once, when Marie was driven almost
to distraction with a six-month bout of rheumatic fever,
sinusitis, and neuralgia, he instinctively brought her the
only thing that could make her feel better: "2 fox terrier
puppies eyes not open yet." And Marie doted on John,

making him shirts, fixing him his favorite meals, worrying about him when he traveled, nursing him during his frequent colds and bouts of flu, his ulcer attacks and stomach distress.

But John and Marie couldn't have been more different. John liked being known as a rancher, but the ranch itself didn't much interest him. What he loved was business, being out in the world, making deals. Marie's idea of heaven might have been a place filled with horses and dogs, but for John it would hardly have been worth the trip unless he could take his checkbook along.

John seldom stayed on the ranch for more than two or three weeks at a time. Then he would be off, down to Mexico with Marie's brother to contract longhorn steers, to New York with his friend Sam on some unspecified business, to Kansas City "with Walker Boys by plane to see Basket Ball Games." Marie occasionally went with him: "Went to San Mateo races with Irene   came over to Oakland to Nims   Grand Time." But almost from the time she left on a trip, she wanted to go home: "Wish I could get home"; "Guess I am poor traveler." "Oh this is a grand day for me   we leave for home tonight   I will never leave again." "Sure was good to get home and best of all everything & everyone seemed glad to see me. What a wonderful place home really is."

More often, John left Marie at home and that suited her fine: "John got off for California   do hope he has a good time & that it does him some good   Sick all day but went to Coconut dance & had grand time   Tom & Irene in." She missed him at times: "letter from John. won't be home for a few days. getting lonesome." But she was philosophical: "Spent my 39th birthday all alone   guess that doesn't make me any older. beautiful day. planting flowers." When he returned, she was simply pleased: "John came home and I was sure glad to see him."

As long as Marie had the ranch, she didn't care what John did. When the ranch was threatened, it was a different matter altogether. John loved risk and he sometimes walked a thin edge. An airline pilot by the name of Slim Lewis financed John in many of his early dealings, and sometimes John became so overextended that Slim wanted more collateral. Shortly after John and Marie bought the Iron Mountain Ranch, Marie wrote: "Slim arrived and wanted my share of ranch so I had to give it up. Maybe for the best   don't think so."

Slim emerged, in the diaries, as a shadow just over the horizon:

JUNE 21, 1939: John home with letter from Slim
don't know what to make of it.

JUNE 30, 1939: I wonder what Slim wants   God
I hope it isn't the ranch

JULY 6, 1939: John & Slim out last night   left
for town this A.M.   back from town late   no deal
with Slim yet

JULY 10, 1939: We talked a good of the ranch &
Slim and the best way for it

Whatever deal John struck, it was temporary, for in November of the next year Marie noted: "John left for town to try & settle with Slim." It's not clear, after that, what arrangements John made, but Marie grew increasingly nervous. Once, when the neighbors kidded John about his precarious finances, it was almost more than Marie could take:

JANUARY 23, 1941: I am really feeling bad over last night's Bridge club at B[eanie's]   They rassed John too much.

FEBRUARY 1, 1941: I do so hate to leave home just scared I will never get back I guess.

FEBRUARY 2, 1941: don't seem to be able to sleep guess I know why.

Then, later that year, Marie learned secondhand that John had made an offer on the Polo Ranch and she was furious: "Mamma says John bought Polo. Well I hope he is happy now but he won't be." John eventually told Marie about the deal and she agreed to sign the mortgage, but with great reluctance:

APRIL 13, 1942: John wants me to sign mortgage on Polo. think it is very bad business.

APRIL 14, 1942: John & I to town to sign 15,000.00 mortgage on Polo   Don't like it very well   We

are getting much too much   Going against my
better judgement

APRIL 15, 1942: Tired after trip to town. Not sure I
should have signed mortgage. Don't know how I
could ever pay it. Another one of those things.

It was a chance to get bigger, but Marie didn't care
about getting bigger. She already had enough; John never
would. This sort of basic difference could tear a relationship
apart. If John had lost the ranch, it probably would have.
He must have understood as much, for though he sometimes found himself in trouble—it's said about him that he
made three fortunes and only lost two—the home ranch
never seemed to be so directly threatened again. Sometimes
a vague nervousness percolated to the surface of Marie's
daily entries: "Hope I never have to leave here." "I love it
here so much, don't know what I would do if I had to
move." But the wolves stayed far enough from the door for
her to simply love the complicated man she had married.

The final year Marie kept a diary, 1963, she seldom wrote.
Her few entries almost all deal with losses. Old Mr. Farth-
ing, Merrill and Tom's father, died; Marie's friend Betty
McCarty's daughter was killed in a car accident; Kennedy
was shot: "Nov 22, 1963: Today our President J. F. Ken-
nedy was shot in Dallas Texas while in a parade   God
Bless & keep him   to me he was a hero & a fine person."
But the death that was hardest on Marie was her dear

friend Irene Farthing. Irene's husband Tom had been Marie's closest friend, and his death from leukemia four years earlier had nearly shattered her: "Why did this have to happen? . . . a big funeral   doing fine til they played The Last Round Up. so very sad." Irene's passing marked Marie's own approaching mortality:

JAN 30, 1963: Irene Farthing died this A.M. at 6:20 I am sure she is much better off   Seems our old gang will soon be together again

FEB 2, 1963: Irenes Funeral this morning at 11. So many deaths this year of people we are fond of. Another chapter closing

The deaths were coming too close together; the entries got further and further apart. Though this last book had room for 1964 and 1965, the pages are blank. Marie set the diary aside for good.

In 1983, Marie had a serious heart attack. I flew down from Montana to be with her. When I arrived, the doctor told me she would not last through the night. She did, and the next night as well, but on the third her kidneys failed and the nurse could find no pulse. Still, she was conscious—barely. The doctor had just been in to see her, and when he left, other members of the family stepped out to talk with him. As I stayed by Marie's bed, they spoke in whispers in the hall, at least fifteen yards from Marie's bed and separated by a half-shut door. I could barely discern their mur-mur, let alone the words. But Marie's eyes opened, and in the sudden acuteness of hearing that visited her, I heard too —they spoke of her death. I tried to talk over it, blubbering nonsense about the weather or the news. Still, she heard. Her jaw jutted forward in the silent gesture I had come to know through the years signaled she had plenty to say but would keep it to herself. In that moment, I believe she steeled her shoulders and decided *not* to die—not there in that sterile hospital, not as a fragile twig of an old lady with a catheter bag hung on her bed. The next day she was stronger, if only slightly, and the doctors were amazed.

I stayed in the hospital room with her for a week. She had no strength to talk, but she liked my being there. Some-times her arms or legs would ache and I would rub them. Her skin was as dry as mica and the bones in her hands seemed as fragile as those of a sparrow, transparent and blue. To pass the time, I'd read to her from the paperback Westerns she loved. She would seem to be sleeping, but once, when I read about a gunman named Tanner, she opened her eyes and said, quite distinctly, "I knew him. He used to ride with my father."

I remember it was April, calving season, and hard crusty snow was spitting against the window behind me. The month had seen one spring blizzard blow in after another. In another hour or two, Floyd and Mel would come in, their faces raw and blistered by wind, their gaits heavy with fatigue. They would tell her about the storms, about the calving, about the ones they had lost and the ones they had saved. They would stand by her side with their hats in their hands, wishing her some piece of their own strength. The book I was reading, like all Westerns, dealt with the passing of the West, and Marie saw her own story in it. But she was not in the book. She was in no Western I had ever read. And she would be the last to ever remark— or even notice—the oversight.

Gradually, Marie regained her strength. In another couple of weeks, she left the hospital to return to the ranch. There she was bed-bound for some time, but with Floyd's help and that of a nurse, she grew strong again. During the summer, the three of them packed into the pickup and drove over the countryside. They watched Quarter Horses being sold in the ring. They visited old friends. Marie said her good-byes from a position of strength. In mid-October, as chill winds came in and the last sere leaves scattered across the ground, Marie made one final trip to town, had a drink with friends, came back to the ranch, and died.

Marie had always been close to her father. "Mama was a wonderful woman, really," she'd say, "but it was Papa who was my friend.

"I'll never forget the time he took me down to see the horses." Marie was just a child then, maybe eight or nine, only slightly older than the twentieth century. The Swan Land and Cattle Company had massed all its horses into one great herd. They held them for the night at the A L. Marie remembered two thousand horses, maybe twenty-five hundred. They completely filled the meadow, over a hundred and sixty acres bounded on two sides by hills and on a third by willow-lined Chugwater Creek.

"Everywhere you looked, as far as you could see," Marie told me, "it was horses. Thousands of horses. A beautiful sight. If I live to be a hundred, I'll never forget it."

She never forgot, either, the night her father died. Earlier in the day she had helped him trail cattle over to Laramie.

"Mama dreamed that something would happen to Dad on that trip," she told me. "She dreamed he would be terribly sick and she would have to take him to the hospital. When he got back, he had three ticks right straight across his stomach. They had all gone in. He got an awful fever, a terrible fever. Mama brought him right to town. It was straight up eleven that night when he died. I was holding his hand.

"Just before he died, he said, 'Marie, there is a horse for you out in Seven Mile Pasture. It is just for you. I want you to have it.' I looked and looked for that horse. But I never found it."

Some part of me suspects that Marie never quit looking for that horse. Marie loved buckskins, but I have always imagined this horse as white or milky grey. It would have to be a ghost horse, glimpsed only in peripheral vision, a flash of a tail disappearing over the rise, an afterimage in a shadow. I imagine she caught fleeting glimpses of it more often as her eyesight failed. And finally, at the end, I imagine Marie peering out from behind her blindness to catch sight of the horse grazing nonchalantly beyond her bed, looking up from time to time to see if she were ready. "Yes," Marie would acknowledge at last with a nod, rising from unconsciousness to catch a grasp of mane and leap up on the great horse's back, graceful even in her flannel night-gown, bounding away from the mortals she loved but trusted would meet up with her later, over the grass and the hills that had been her life, over her herds of Herefords, through the grey misty clouds to the glittering meadow where all her dogs and horses, all her family and friends, would be waiting for her to come through the gate, riding the white horse home.

The Death
of the Hired Man

Leonard Cheser, the foreman of our ranch for many years

When I was little, an old man by the name of Kelley worked for us. He was not a cowboy, which is to say he didn't ride. Rather, he was the chore boy, which meant he did everything else. He tended the garden, cut the lawn, milked the cow, fed the chickens, sharpened sickles for the mowing machine, carpentered, plumbed, and fixed fence. Above all, he irrigated. He had an eye for incline and gravity, and in a country where water was precious, he made it go a long way. I once heard it said that Kelley could run water up a witch's tit. Even my grandfather, seldom bent to a compliment, said Kelley was the only one who really understood water on the Jordan Ranch.

Kelley was my friend. He took me with him everywhere and I loved him. He never talked much, but he chuckled when I said something clever and he let me shift the Jeep while he clutched.

I have a hard time visualizing him now. Small details come into focus—his heavy lace-up work boots, the frayed cuffs of his Levi's, his flannel shirts, the flash of red from his pouch of Beech-Nut chewing tobacco—but I can't remember his face. It's almost as if I were too small to step back and take him in whole. Mostly, I remember his hands, the pure white hair on the backs of his broad stubby fingers, the cracked thumbnails imbedded with fine dark lines, the deep scab on the break of one knuckle, the blue veins that rose so distinctly as he gripped a shovel handle or a steering wheel.

His hands were always in motion and there was something rhythmic about them. I loved to watch him sharpen sickles. The sharpening wheel sat in the darkest part of the barn, and each time Kelley brought one of the triangular blades to the wheel, sparks flew in an arc. I could watch that curve of orange stars for hours, and the sweet, sweeeet, sweeeet whine of metal against stone would draw me from wherever I might be playing to take up my seat on a milking stool in the cool shadows. I was a talkative kid, but I kept my silence when Kelley sharpened sickles. The action, so musical and meditative, had the power to cast even me in its spell.

Kelley introduced me to the elemental world. He was the one my brother Blade and I would tell when we found a bull snake. Bull snakes, with their appetite for mice, were precious. "Kelley!" we would yell. "We found you a snake!" The old man would come and peer at it for a moment and then lean down as if to regard it closer. Suddenly, with a motion as quick as a cat's, he would grab it behind the head. Then he would be all slowness and calm again and the bull snake would wrap itself around his arm as if even it knew there was no reason to be afraid. Blade and I would follow Kelley down to the cake shack, the old boxcar on blocks where we stored concentrated feed for the cattle. The dark shack smelled of dust and grain and molasses; sacks of cottonseed cake were stacked up to the ceiling and mouse droppings were scattered everywhere. We would release the bull snake and say, "Good hunting, old fellow. Have a good time."

The first time I caught a bull snake by myself, I ran to Kelley shouting, "Look what I did, Kelley, look what I did!" The snake was big, five or six feet long. It wrapped itself tightly around my arm. I can still feel its muscular grip and the warmth it had picked up from the sun. Kelley nodded appreciatively. "This time," he said, "I'll walk *you* to the cake shack."

Everything Kelley did fascinated me. He fashioned a latch for the chicken coop from a piece of willow and a leather thong. He notched corral poles with a hatchet. He spaded manure into watertight dams, threaded earthworms on hooks, gutted trout, ran his traps.

One night I helped him skin three beavers. Kelley pulled them up from the water and laid them out on the ground. The largest was nearly as big as I was—I must have been five at the time. All three were dark and shiny and had a sense of great mass, something both sad and majestic. I remember wanting to lie down next to them, to cuddle up, to sleep. Kelley squatted next to the largest one for a long time, stroking its dead forehead as he might a dog's.

We skinned out the two smaller ones. My job was to pull back on the pelt as Kelley cut it away from the carcass, and I'd watch the deft flash of his knife as he worked in the moonlight. When he cut into the big beaver, he punctured the bile. The smell was immediate and overpowering— green, black, utterly wretched. I tried to concentrate on other things—the sound of frogs along the creek, the prospect of a trip to town the next day with my mother—but all I wanted to do was cry. Instead, I leaned back as far as I could and tried not to breathe at all. Kelley skinned at arms' length and finally we finished. He threw the pelts into the back of the Jeep and left the carcasses for the coyotes. We got in and he nodded for me to work the gearshift. I shifted into second. When the Jeep jerked forward, he said, "You're a trooper." He reached into his pocket and brought out a smooth stone. "Here. I found this today." When I got it home under the light, I saw it was sky blue, the color of a robin's egg.

Kelley had a weakness for liquor. He never drank on the ranch. He could have; there was no rule against it. What a man did on his own time was of no concern as long as he turned up sober for work. But Kelley knew that if he took one drink, he was lost. He could stay dry for months at a time, ordering the small extras he wanted from my mother when she went to town: Beech-Nut tobacco, Black Jack gum. But sooner or later he'd get an itch. He'd draw his wages and we wouldn't see him for three or four days, sometimes five. When he'd return, his stubble of beard would have a yellow tint and he'd smell different, sour and old. I'd run up to him like I always did and he'd ruffle my hair, but he wouldn't look me in the eye. He'd talk to my father then, holding his hat in front of him with both hands, fidgeting with its brim. Few words passed between them. They had a perfect understanding. Kelley was welcome here until he started drinking, and then he wasn't.

Usually, when Kelley left us, he'd go to work for the Diamond, a ranch twenty miles further down Chugwater Creek. There he'd stay until his semiannual thirst bounced him back to us. Kelley was a good hand. If my father had a spot for him, he always hired him back.

Until the day he didn't. The last time Kelley came to the door for a job, his eyes were sallow, red in the corners, and there was a sunken look about him. Even the hair on the back of his hands had a yellowish tinge. It was almost noon, but my father hadn't come in yet. My mother sat Kelley down at the kitchen table and gave him a cup of coffee. I bounced down beside him. He gave me a weak grin as he cradled his coffee cup in both hands to keep it from shaking. "How you doin', kid," he said.

My father came in for lunch and he and Kelley went to the desk in the corner of the dining room. I sat on the stairs, half-hidden by the rail, to watch the transaction, the small advance, that would mean my friend was back in my life. There was much low talking and shaking of heads. Nothing changed hands. My father walked Kelley to the door. I stood at the kitchen window and watched him drive off in his little topless Jeep, a single satchel and a few traps in the back, his shoulders hunched to the wheel.

Nearly 7 million ranch and farm jobs have disappeared since 1950. Over 5.5 million of those belonged to family members who lost their jobs when they lost their land, but about 1.5 million wage jobs have disappeared as well. Our own ranch is typical. When I was a child, we hired four or five men and a cook year-round. In the summer, for haying, we hired five or six more—"good" drunks like Kelley who could dry out for a while and knew how to do things; the younger brothers of men who already worked for us; college kids from all over the country who learned about us one way or another.

The hay crew consisted of two men who drove mowers, two men on rakes (to gather the hay into windrows), two men on sweeps (to push the windrows into small stacks), one man on a hydraulic stacker (to lift the small stacks into a large one in a fenced enclosure called a stack lot), and one or two men on the stack with pitchforks to arrange the hay so it was stable and weather-tight. In addition, one man stayed horseback all summer and took care of the cattle, and the choreboy took care of everything else.

I've always wished I had been born in time to see haying with horses, but there was a splendid choreography to haying as I knew it, the mowers and rakes and sweeps scurrying all along the meadow, the stacker backing up to get a load and then lifting it high to dump it on the stack, the stack man rearranging great forkfuls of hay in an ancient art.

But these men were soon to become obsolete. By the time our ranch was sold, my father and two men did the year-round work; we hired one extra person for the summer. Haying had become a three-man show: one man on the windrower, which cut, crimped, and left the hay in windrows; one man on the round baler, which drove down the windrows and spat out one-ton bales; and one man on the Haymaster to carry the bales into the stack lot. We no longer needed a chore boy—we bought eggs, milk, vegetables, and even meat in town, and whoever ran the Haymaster could irrigate. We no longer needed a cook—we hired only married men.

In earlier years, the ranch had been its own community. Our foreman and his family lived at the J T, another man and his family lived at the A L. If the cook was married, her husband worked for us, too. The cook fed my grandfather and the two or three single men who lived in the bunkhouse. During haying, five or six more men lived above the garage. If the married men were working at the main place, the cook fed them too, as well as anyone else who turned up hungry.

There was a definite hierarchy on the ranch, and its parameters were simple—skill and a sense of responsibility. The top hands were the cowboys, generally married men, who stayed with us for years and worked their way up to foreman: Harold McSkimmon, Andy Shaeffer, Jay Horsman, Harold Dunkin, Nelson Vineyard, Leonard Cheser. Then came the single men who could handle horses and machines. I remember Sammy Allen, the first person I ever met who was in a good mood all the time. My brother and I loved to work with him because he never, but never, got mad. Besides, he had an inexhaustible supply of jokes. His brothers Dan and Jay worked for us from time to time, too.

Next in line came the chore boy, usually an old man like Kelley. At the bottom of the heap were the blowhards. One called himself Buffalo Bob and told us that he was such a famous bronc rider he'd had to change his name to escape his fans. His sort didn't last long. The other men usually ran them off before they messed up badly enough to get fired.

Every ranch wears a patina of stories about the men and women who once worked there. I grew up hearing about Jay Miller. He didn't have any teeth and every so often he'd make an appointment with the dentist. But dentists made him nervous, and each time he went to town for an appointment, he'd stop in the bar to take the edge off. He'd drink up his paycheck and he still wouldn't have any teeth. Finally, he clipped a mail-order ad out of a magazine. He sent in the coupon for a kit to make a mold. He mixed up the plaster of Paris but forgot to grease his gums. He chomped down and the mold stuck fast.

When his gums healed, he sent off again, and this time he remembered the Crisco and the mold worked fine. He sent it in and in a few weeks received his teeth. He was proud of them, even though they hurt him some. One day he and my grandfather were horseback several miles from the house when Jay's horse went to bucking and dumped him in a snowdrift. "Damn!" he said as he picked himself up. "I lost my teeth." My grandfather, who had followed the progress of those teeth for a couple of years, climbed off his horse and the two of them dug around in the snow for an hour without any luck. Finally, they gave up and rode home. At dinnertime, Jay showed up with his teeth. "Where the hell'd you get those?" my grandfather demanded.

"From the glass by the sink," Jay answered with a shrug.

There were the sad cases such as Carl, a chore boy who always said "Halloo, halloo, halloo." He never received mail except for catalogues from Frederick's of Hollywood until he returned from a weekend in town. Then, for a few days, he would receive thick letters. One time a cook got curious and steamed one open. It contained nothing but sheets of folded-up newspaper. My father fired him when my brother and I came along. "There was something wrong with his he-she stuff," my father told me. "I didn't know what it was, but I didn't want him around my kids."

The ranch saw plenty of heartbreak. One time a fellow reached up into the teeth of his scatter rake to clear out compacted hay and a rattlesnake bit him. It was early in the day, but he didn't say anything until noon. By that time he was pretty sick and then he had a reaction to the antivenom and almost died. A couple of weeks later, when he got out of the hospital, he came home to find that one of the other men had moved in with his wife.

I remember a single man in his fifties named Armand.

He arrived in a Western sports coat, not new but clean and well cut, and a decent pair of boots. He had his own saddle and a couple of suitcases full of clothes. All good signs. He was a good hand, too, quiet and competent. Pretty soon there seemed to be a spark between him and Mickie, the cook. Mickie deserved a little happiness and everyone was pleased. Armand proposed and they seemed happy. Then one day, after about a year, Armand disappeared. The ranch pickup he'd been driving was found off the side of the road just a few miles from the house. There was no indication he'd run off—his saddle was in the barn, his clothes were in the closet, and even the small bills he usually left on the top of the dresser were undisturbed. We were all certain he'd come to harm. "He was so good-hearted," Mickie told my mother. "He must have stopped to help somebody and they did him in. If he's left me, I'll never trust another living human." Nothing turned up for a year or so, and then an FBI man drove in with the information that Armand had a string of wives in a dozen states. Mickie took to drinking and pretty soon she headed down the road.

Drink caused its share of problems on the ranch. Part of the cook's job was to clean my grandfather's apartment, and one cook decided to help herself to a bottle of his whiskey. By dinnertime she had made quite a dent in it. She was in such a generous mood that she offered Sunny a drink. My grandfather never refused a drink, but it made him mad to be offered his own whiskey, so he wrote out her check. She was still pretty tight when my father drove her to town and she cussed him the whole way. "You're so dumb," she yelled at one point, "you couldn't pour piss out of a boot if the directions were writ on the heel."

Ray and Evelyn Orange worked for us when I was very young. Ray got cancer in his shoulder and I remember how the orange salve he was given for treatment soaked through his shirt. It had an acrid smell and in my mind cancer will always be associated with the color orange.

A short, round woman by the name of Mrs. Lewis cooked for years. The hay crew always came in for lunch at noon, but if people were horseback and ran into trouble, they could be hours late. Mrs. Lewis had a sixth sense. No matter what time somebody rode in, she had a steak and French fries hot on the table for him. She made her own noodles and I loved to watch her throw flour on the board in a perfect arc. She'd roll a ball of dough into a thin sheet in a few deft strokes, then cut the noodles with a six-wheeled roller. Her stainless-steel gravy spoon hung on a hook beside the stove. Its bowl was as big as the palm of a man's hand, but worn off at a sharp angle on one side from stirring. She wrote stories for *True Confessions* and her little Royal typewriter always sat at the end of the table.

The real royalty of the ranch, though, were the long-time married men. Nelson Vineyard, his wife Carolyn, and their two sons, Guy and Tod, came to the ranch in 1958. They lived first at the A L and then, after Nelson had been promoted to foreman, at the J T. Guy and Tod were just younger than Blade and I; two more boys, Rodney and Mike, were born while they lived on the ranch. We often stayed at each other's houses, we went to the one-room school together, we rode all over the country and got into no end of trouble.

There has never been phone service between the main ranch and the A L and the dirt road that connects the two places often drifts closed in the winter. Nelson fed the cows on his end of the ranch alone, and sometimes he wouldn't see my father or Sunny for two or three weeks at a time. He loaded the hay sled each day by "needling" the hay, rigging a system of pipes and chains to flip the hay from the stack to the sled with a minimum of effort. He once did a caesarian on a cow by following the directions in a book. "I had the same tools as a vet did in those days," he told me, "a pair of rubber gloves and a bucket with a hose in it. But if I hadn't done something, the cow would have died.

"I didn't always do things the way your Dad or Sunny would have," he added, "but they let me do it my way. There was always the understanding that we were working for the same things."

Blade and I thought Nelson was the most handsome man we had ever met—he looked just like Eric Fleming, the trail boss in *Rawhide*. My father respected him for more prosaic reasons. "I'll tell you what sort of man Nelson is," my father said when I asked him. "After the Vineyards had been here for several years, Nelson found a better job. He told me far in advance, and if he had found something that would get him along, I was happy for him. We were calving, and he said he would stay until he'd calved out the two-year olds. We set a date which gave us plenty of time. As the day approached, there were still a few heifers to calve out. Then there were two. And then, on the day he was set to leave, there was one. The Vineyards packed the car and then Nelson went down to check the heifer. He called me and said that she didn't look ready. I said 'You go on ahead. I'll be up at eleven o'clock to check on her; don't worry.' I got up there about ten-thirty and Nelson had just pulled the calf. His going-to-town clothes were hung up on the fence, and he was practically naked. They'd been headed out the driveway and he thought, 'No, I'll just check her one more time.' He'd already signed off with me and I would have been up there long before the calf would have been in trouble. But he went back to check one more time."

The Vineyards left when I was twelve and Leonard and Lila Cheser and their four children, Dan, Tim, Mike, and Roxanne, came soon after. They stayed on the ranch until it was sold in 1978; I became an adult while they were there.

When I think about Leonard, I think of J. Frank Dobie's measure of a man: "The best you can say is he's good to his horse and the worst you can say is he ain't." Leonard was a good man. His horses always came first. He and Lila arrived with a mare named Chub and a gelding named Bill. Leonard babied them and they'd do anything for him. He had trained cutting horses for a fellow in North Dakota and he can put as good a rein on a horse as anyone I know.

The last summer we had the ranch, I worked for Leonard. My father had just remarried and was often away; a couple of times a week I had supper with Leonard and Lila or came down to their house later to visit. By that time, their son Dan worked for us and sometimes he and his wife Nina came down in the evenings, too.

Leonard looks sort of like Gary Cooper, tall and lanky, maybe six feet two, 140 pounds. He grew up in North Dakota—he always just said "Dakota"—on his father's ranch, in a world entirely defined by horses. "The way Dad made his money," Leonard told me, "was breaking horses. He'd go to the sale ring and buy these spoiled horses and unbroke two- and three-year olds. He'd bring them home, and we'd break them during the winter and sell them in the spring.

"Dad was big. I've always been sort of skinny but Dad —six foot five, maybe six foot six, two-hundred and seventy pounds. He would rope 'em and snub 'em, saddle 'em, blindfold 'em. I'd walk up and he'd just kind of take me by the arm and boost me up. When I hit the saddle, he'd pull the blindfold off. After you get throwed off four or five times, you'd think you had enough, but he'd always say, 'Lots of daylight left'—he always went by daylight—'we can ride one or two yet today.' "

Leonard learned to ride broncs, train cow ponies, and break eight-horse teams to the three-bottom plow. And then, when he was thirteen, his father died.

"We had gone out to fix a windmill. I was up on the tower and I needed to pull up a couple of two-by-fours. I'd dropped the rope for the first one. Dad tied it on and I pulled it up. I dropped the rope for the second one. He was standing there, kind of leaning against the windmill. I waited for him to tie on the second two-by-four, but he didn't grab hold of the rope. I called down to him: "Dad, aren't you going to tie that rope?' No answer, so I hollered louder. I thought he didn't hear me. I climbed down to see what was the matter. When I got on the ground, I reached over to touch him. I said, 'Dad,' and he fell flat on his face, stone dead. The coroner said it was a heart attack.

"The ranch was big enough—we farmed about three sections and had another twelve sections of hay and pastureland—but it was the Depression and everything was mortgaged. We just gathered everything together and had a big auction sale and the family pretty much scattered after that."

Leonard didn't get along with his mother and he went to work for an uncle. "He was a hard one," Leonard recalled. "Most people treat their dogs better." When the uncle sent Leonard out during a lightning storm with a wheelbarrow full of posts and wire to fix fences, Leonard ditched the wheelbarrow in a draw and hit the road. He was on his own from then on. He never finished eighth grade.

He joined the army when he was seventeen and served as a machine gunner in Europe during World War II. When the war was over, he returned to "Dakota" and worked for the Parks Department in Jamestown, building roads, planting trees, and running the ice-skating rinks. He courted Lila for several years before they finally got married, and they have worked on ranches ever since.

"My first love is a horse," Leonard told me, "but I like cattle, I just love to mess with cattle. I suppose that's what makes it so easy for me to calve heifers. And I suppose that's one way to get to mess with a horse, to mess with cattle."

Leonard is a good mechanic, though he swears he hates it. "I don't mind being up to my ears in manure, but I hate to get grease on my hands." Still, he kept the windrower and baler, both complicated machines, humming. "A baler's like a woman," he once told me, "awful touchy. Treat her gentle, though, and everything is sweet."

A good cowboy needs to be a horseman, a vet, a midwife, a mechanic, a carpenter, a plumber, a surveyor, and an electrician. The pay isn't much for all these skills. When we sold the ranch, Leonard received $600 a month—that would be equivalent to about $1,200 in 1990. On top of that, he had his house and utilities furnished, and all the beef he could eat. He had pasture and feed for his horses and the right, if he wanted, to run a few cattle of his own. The ranch would match contributions for health insurance and a pension fund for anyone who had been with us over a year, but few cowboys accepted it.

"You might be able to make more working in town," Leonard told me once. "I suppose if I belonged to a union, making cars or something, I'd be making a lot more. But the thing about this work is that it is never routine, it never gets boring. Calving can be hellish hard and you get dead tired, but it's exciting, too. Everyday those little babies hitting the ground. And in six, seven weeks, it's over. Then you move cattle to high ground, you brand. Haying gets monotonous, but in four or six weeks that's over and then you're back to cattle work, gathering and weaning and shipping. In the winter, you're done feeding by eleven, eleven-thirty in the morning, and if everything goes well, you have the rest of the day to yourself. Then comes calving and you're working around the clock. No two days are ever the same and nobody is standing over you, telling you how to do it.

"Your dad—him and I, we got mad sometimes, we both got mad. But we knew just exactly how far we could push each other. We either walked off or we just let it go."

This world of hired men has shrunk until it is nearly non-existent. The rural economy once supported millions of people. There were jobs on farms and ranches and, because there were people in the country, there were also schools and stores and post offices. There was room for real professionals like Nelson and Leonard and room for the Kelleys of the world.

Nelson has worked for the gas company in Wheatland since he left our ranch. Carolyn, who once confided to my mother that she worried about Nelson's health because she didn't know how she could support the boys, earned her G.E.D. and went to college and now has a successful day-care business. Still, they have often thought of returning to the land. "Nelson loved calving, that time in the spring when everything was new," Carolyn told me last time I talked with her. "Now, every March he gets moody." Their oldest son, Guy, learned his profession working at his father's side and now runs a ranch with his wife in northern Wyoming. Nelson and Carolyn had a fifth son after they moved to town. "Dave has always felt that his brothers got something he didn't."

Leonard and Lila worked on one more ranch after ours

and then retired—if you can call it that. Leonard, now in his late sixties, won't give up working with horses and cattle and hires out for day work, often helping his son Dan, who is foreman of a ranch near Chugwater. Lila, who taught herself how to reupholster furniture and refinish antiques, has plenty of business.

Kelley was lucky, in a way, to be getting old when he did. He was so broken down near the end that no one would hire him. But he'd worked all his life and he had Social Security to live on. He retired to Chugwater and raised a big garden until age and drink caught up with him.

The Burnside area of Portland, the city's skid row, is filled with men like Kelley. "This used to clear out in the summer," a social worker told me a couple of years ago. "Everyone would head out to farms and ranches. But now those jobs are gone." Some can adapt, but a man like Kelley could never flip burgers at Wendy's. He was flawed, but he had dignity, he had skills and artistry, he paid his own way. There was a place for him in the county; there is no place for him now.

Writing
My Grandmother's Life

Effie during her college years

In the first photograph I have of my grandmother, she is reaching for something. Eight months old, she wears a christening gown of Irish lace and sits on a Persian rug. She is smiling and her large brown eyes show not the astonishment common in infant expressions but something more: something deep, intelligent, intensely present. Still, it is her hand, that grasping hand, that most intrigues me. What is she reaching for? The camera? The diamond of light reflected in the photographer's spectacles? Her arm stretches its full length, but three fingers curl to the palm as if to deny the reach. As if she knows, already, that a woman can ask for too much.

The woman I called Gran did not resemble this endearing infant. Effie Lannen Jordan was what was known politely as a "difficult woman." She lived in the same community all her life, but I have never heard an affectionate story about her. She managed to undermine even her generous impulses. When she gave my brother and me gifts, she would announce we were to come to her apartment to receive them. If we came too quickly, we were greedy. If we came too slowly, we showed disrespect. Nor could we thank her properly. If we wrote a note right away, we were fishing for more. And if we wrote too slowly—or God forbid, not at all—we were ungrateful.

Effie died at the age of eighty-three with only two accomplishments: she had raised a son and completed needlepoint seat covers for a dozen dining-room chairs. Her son, my father, cannot remember a single comfortable moment spent in her company, and the needlepoint, my grandmother always complained, had ruined her beautiful eyes.

For years, I seldom mentioned my grandmother—why talk about such bitterness? But a few years after her death, I was stalled on a project I had worked on for years. The frustration was familiar—I'd had trouble completing projects before. Unable to finish, unwilling to give up, I saw life passing me by. During the midst of this personal hell, I had a dream, and it was this dream that made me think about my grandmother's life.

In the dream, twin girls lived in an old Victorian house. The girls were six or seven years old and they wore white dresses. Their hair was tied back and they were pretty, yet sad. They never spoke. The interior of the house was murky and dark: the girls' dresses seemed to glow.

A set of railroad tracks passed through the house. A post about four feet high stood on either side of the tracks with an electric eye mounted on top of each post. A beam of light passed between the two eyes.

When the girls heard the train, their job was to run to the posts and hold their fingers in front of the electric eyes to break the beam. If they failed, the train would come to a crashing halt. Their job was to see that this never happened.

A train came rushing through. The girls were at their stations, and the passage was very pretty, very eerie: the line of the headlight piercing the murkiness and illuminating the girls in their white dresses; the shadows from the girls' fingers dancing in the mist; the way the train, so fast and streamlined, rushed through on its shimmering wheels, dust and steam roiling all around. The girls stood close to the train, frightened yet excited by the knowledge that people were being swept past to fascinating and unimaginable lives. With the train between them, the girls couldn't see one another. When it disappeared into the night, they receded back into their shadowy silence.

A second train approached, but this time the girls didn't get to the electric eyes in time and the beam stretched across the tracks unbroken. The engine smashed into it, grinding to a screeching halt, all the cars buckling up behind. Sparks flew everywhere and the air filled with the smell of scorched metal. The girls couldn't see one another but they both knew that they had done something terribly wrong.

The dream carried one final image. The doors to the cars were open. The girls could get on the train if they wanted to. Everything was quiet again. As long as the train stood still, its open doors beckoning, the girls couldn't see one another.

I woke with the knowledge that I had had an Important Dream. I didn't know who the girls were. Only the dresses were familiar, those turn-of-the-century white dresses with broad sashes and lace trim. In my attic, I had a half-dozen apple boxes filled with family photographs. Among the photographs were pictures of girls dressed in white.

I dug out the boxes and found a picture of my grandmother at the age of three, wearing a white dress. I found, too, a snapshot of myself at the same age, taken in my grandmother's apartment. I was wearing white flannel pajamas with ribbon trim. I set the two photographs side by side. We looked exactly alike. We could have been twins. This recognition did nothing to comfort me. The worst insult one member of my family could hurtle at another was "You are just like Gran."

Gran: even the word seemed acid and thin. Through the years, I had tried to eradicate anything about myself that might recall her. She was lethargic; I hardly ever sat down. She was critical; I was complimentary, sometimes to the point of obsequiousness. She never forgot a slight; I never held a grudge. My greatest fear had always been that Gran would somehow manifest herself in me, that I was condemned, as if genetically, to her bitterness and lethargy. I sometimes caught myself at the mirror, trying to reassure myself that I bore no trace of her cynical sneer, her perpetual pout.

In my memory, Gran was a witch: ugly and mean. But I looked at her picture at age three. She wasn't a witch then. She was beautiful, endearing, charismatic. Something had happened.

I pawed through the boxes and pulled out every photograph of my grandmother. I set them out on my dining-room table and arranged them in chronological order. In the earliest pictures, Effie's hands grabbed my attention. First was that christening photograph, taken at three months, where she reached for something. In the next picture, at one-and-a-half years, she stood between her parents, supported by her father's arm. She looked directly into the camera—again, those clear, perceptive eyes—and she held onto her own ear as if to say, "This is mine." In a third photograph, taken at age three, her hands rested passively, one in her lap and the other at her side, but she looked into the camera with complete openness and with something I could only describe as knowingness. I was struck by the personality present in those early photographs, and by the undercurrent of mirth. And I noticed, too, how joy and accessibility never surfaced again.

At five, she was photographed once again with her parents, and this time a sense of wariness had come into her eyes. They still shone, but they knew something—they had seen something—that they hadn't before. They revealed reticence, self-consciousness. I recognized, too, the beginning of a tightness around the mouth that she would wear the rest of her life.

At seven or eight, Effie was once again photographed alone, in another white dress. She had a child's body, but the face could have belonged to someone much older. She wore a measure of determination and perhaps of rebellion. This was the first photograph where the pose seemed obvious, an important turning point, I suppose, for a woman who would become known as a great *poseur*.

Two school photos—sad, resigned, wary. Then came a series of six photographs matted in a single frame, taken with her much younger sister, my Great-aunt Marj. Effie must have been about fifteen and Marjorie five. Both girls wore beautiful white dresses. Effie was alone in the first and last pictures, playing the piano. In the first, she looked at the camera, the tightness around her mouth bent into a smile. In the last, she leaned to her music in what seemed a parody of concentration. Almost all the photographs seemed staged. In three of the shots with Marj, the toddler seemed but a prop against which Effie could play good sister. But in one photograph, Effie's mask was completely absent and she seemed as guileless as she had in her earliest portraits, but ever so much sadder.

Then there were the photographs taken during college at the University of Kansas. Here Effie was all style and attitude. In one, with a cloche, she looked like an Inuit. In another, hand cocked on hip and outrageous, corded "cap," she looked like a flapper. And in a third, dark-brimmed hat pulled low over her sensuous eyes, she had the sultry elegance of a film star. Each portrait seemed distinct, as if a separate personality resided behind its ruse.

Effie never finished college. She always became "too ill"

to take exams. She returned to Cheyenne and married my grandfather, Sunny. No wedding photographs have survived. Probably, she burnt them in one of her periodic fits of rage against the man she would neither live with nor divorce for forty years of a fifty-year marriage.

The visual chronicle picked up again in the mid-twenties and showed a change so pronounced as to be shocking. Gone was all the stylishness, the air. A formal portrait revealed a rather plain woman with a look of defeat. The snapshots from the era were even more disturbing. Several showed her in 1928 with her newborn baby, Larry, my father. Effie looked fifty years old. She was twenty-seven. She smiled in the photos, but it was a pained sort of smile. I tried to figure out why she looked so awkward and finally it came to me. She nestled the baby against her right breast. Most women, even left-handed ones, hold their babies close to the heart. In another photo, she tried to adjust the baby's sweater and her clumsiness was painful. Even when she held her son in his christening gown when he was eight months old, she looked like she had never held a child before.

And then there was the Christmas photo with the family, one of the rare photographs that showed Effie and Sunny together. The tree glittered in the background, but Effie slumped in her chair in an attitude of utter defeat, Sunny looked at the camera with a wry tenseness, Effie's sister Marj was almost hidden—as she was in most family photographs—and seemed to be trying to appear pleasant, and Marj and Effie's parents, Nana and Papa Dick, sat stiffly in their chairs. Little Larry, six or seven years old, sat on the floor inspecting his new rifle, but even this activity brought no joy. He looked absorbed but miserable, as if wishing only for escape.

The visual record skipped the forties. The next photograph was taken at the same time as portraits of Nana and Marj. By this time, Marj's marriage had ended in divorce and all three women lived together in Cheyenne. My grandmother looked ineffably sad. The three women were together again in the next photo, taken in 1960. This was the Gran I knew, sharp and witchlike, with something truly nasty in her face. Finally, the last photos, taken at my father's second wedding in 1977: Effie was short and shrunken, but in one picture she was actually laughing. In nearly eighty years of photographs, this was the only one that caught her laughing. I knew that laugh, that bitter laugh: it was her witch's cackle.

There is danger in reading too much into snapshots, but I felt safe in drawing a few conclusions. Effie was born with a personality that tended more to the active than the passive; she had some desire to make a mark or at least be noticed; she did not fare well in marriage; and she was almost crazy with unhappiness.

"Lives do not serve as models," wrote Carolyn Heilbrun in her landmark study of women's biographies and autobiographies, *Writing a Woman's Life*. "Only stories do that. We can only retell and live by the stories we have read or heard. They may be read, or chanted, or experienced electronically, or come to us, like the murmurings of our mothers, telling us what conventions demand. Whatever their form or medium, these stories have formed us all. . . ."

Was there some clue to my grandmother in the stories that shaped her, the stories that shaped women of her time? As Heilbrun noted, until recently a woman had only one primary story to live by and it instructed her to put a man at the center of her life "and . . . allow to occur only what honors his prime position. Occasionally, women have put God or Christ [or social work or teaching] in the place of a man; the results are the same: one's own desires and quests are always secondary. For a short time, during courtship, the illusion is maintained that women, by withholding themselves, are central. . . . And courtship itself is, as often as not, an illusion: that is, the woman must entrap the man to ensure herself a center for her life. The rest is aging and regret."

Aging and regret: surely, that described Effie's life after marriage. My grandmother did not put her husband at the center of her life; she never put anyone at the center of her life except herself. She was criticized for this; she was also dreadfully unhappy and she made everyone around her unhappy as well. For the first time, I began to have sympathy for my grandmother. What if she didn't *want* to put someone else at the center of her life? What if she were virtually incapable of it? She had been, after all, a child with a distinct personality, an infant who held on to her own ear. What if she wanted something that was uniquely hers? It's possible to imagine a woman my age making this choice and having a rich and admirable life. It was virtually *impossible* to imagine a woman—at least a conventional woman —in Effie's time doing so.

There were, of course, women of achievement whom Effie would have been familiar with—George Sand, George Eliot, and Jane Addams in the nineteenth century, Eleanor Roosevelt and Dorothy Day in the twentieth, to name a few. But the stories that were available to Effie about these women did little to provide her with alternatives for her own life. Many of them released themselves from conventional expectations only by doing something outrageous—the writer George Eliot, for instance, lived openly with a married man. Such audacity was unthinkable for my grandmother. At least by the time I knew her, she was appalled by any breach of "proper" conduct. My failure to carry the appropriate purse for my shoes would throw her into a rage, as would a daring hair style on one of her peers.

Effie had learned early to fear unrestrained behavior. She had been born in 1900 and raised on my great-grandparents' ranch, the L T, twenty-five miles north of Cheyenne. Her father, David Lannen—the family called him Papa Dick—was handsome and a bit of a rogue. At least one paternity suit was threatened against him if not actually filed, and he was rumored to have a bastard son. Certainly, he drank.

Papa Dick was decisive. He was said to have killed two men when he found a pair of his steers dead in the back of their wagon."Papa Dick's L T brand was right on top" is the way my father tells the story. "The rustlers were so lazy they hadn't even skinned 'em out." So my great-grandfather shot them. In the parlance of the country, they "needed killing." They were found with stones under their heads, supposedly a trademark of the stock detective Tom Horn. Horn was glad to take the credit—a hired gun will always add another notch or two to the résumé. Or so the story goes.

But it was Nana who had the strength in the family— or so *that* story goes. Nana was sixteen years younger than Papa Dick and she took on more and more responsibility as he grew older. Papa Dick's health "failed"—family stories aren't clear exactly how. It might have been asthma or depression or fatigue. Possibly, it was related to alcohol. Whatever the cause, Nana was said to do all the work, at least during the last few years on the ranch. They sold out in 1914 and moved to town.

Nana prevailed in other ways as well. Papa Dick was Irish Catholic but Nana was Scotch Presbyterian and raised the girls in her faith. Gran and Marj grew into rabid anti-Catholics. And when Papa Dick lay on his deathbed in 1939 and asked for last rites, Nana wouldn't let the priest through the door.

Order was important to Nana, and so was propriety. I can only imagine the scenes that took place when Papa Dick came home tipsy. And I shudder to think what happened when he was accused of philandering. Nana convinced the woman who had been caught in a family way to drop her suit—and knowing Nana, I suspect she did not employ the most gentle forms of persuasion. I suspect, too, that Effie and Marj learned at an early age that indiscretion threatened to unravel the very fabric of their lives.

Unconventionality was not the only option open to my grandmother. Many women had succeeded while living apparently within convention. Still, they did not provide stories my grandmother or other women could live by, because the stories available about them did not reveal the truths of their lives. Eleanor Roosevelt's life stood as an extraordinary model of achievement, but the *story* of her life stressed that she took up her work only to help her husband—"doctors urged her to busy herself with a career in part to encourage [her husband] to involve himself again with the world around him [after he was stricken with polio in 1921]." As Heilbrun pointed out, "Well into the twentieth century, it continued to be impossible for women to admit into their autobiographical narratives the claim of achievement, the admission of ambition, the recognition that accomplishment was neither luck nor the result of the efforts or generosity of others. . . . Each woman set out to find her life's work, but the only script insisted that work discover and pursue her, like the conventional romantic lover."

I always had the feeling that Effie was angry at the world for not making her happy; I was angry at Effie for not making *herself* happy. I realize now that she didn't have the slightest idea what she wanted. Nothing she had seen or heard told her that her happiness was her own responsibility or that, if the conventional life did not satisfy her, she should search for one that did. No wonder she was crotchety.

Would she have been happier had she been raised with

other possibilities? She was extremely intelligent—she had an incisive wit, played a wicked hand of bridge, and would regularly recall entire passages from *Wall Street Journal* articles she had read weeks before. She quite possibly had other talents as well. John Briggs, in *Fire in the Crucible,* a study of creative genius, notes the necessity of coincidence for talent to flourish: "A computer prodigy born into a culture where there are no computers or a musical prodigy born into a family where music is forbidden would be like sparks falling into the desert.... Most often, however, the prodigy's special spark is 'lost' because it finds no tinder...." My grandmother was not a prodigy, but coincidence is necessary for more modest talents as well. Whatever embers she possessed fell in a desert where they did not extinguish so much as smolder until they marked her and everything she touched.

If she had been a man born to similar class and circumstance, she could have strode out into the world and taken hold of something that satisfied her; as a woman, she was instructed to remain passive. Everyone who talks about Gran says, "She really thought she was something, didn't she?" and they say it—each member of my family has said it, I have said it—with a tone of anger and bitterness. Who did she think she was to think she was so great? I have seldom heard this tone of voice applied to a man—a man who thought he was something could go out and *become* something. The only thing Effie could become was the wife of a man who was something. Her culture instructed her to stand mute in the shadows and make it possible for someone else's train to speed through.

It's easy to be angry at her for not "making the best of the situation," finding a way to be happy within marriage or club work or social causes. So very many women did. And yet many women didn't. As I began to talk about my grandmother, I was constantly told "I had a grandmother like that," or "You are writing about my great-aunt." One out of five women my age will never marry. Demographics play a role, but a good number of contemporary women *choose* not to marry because marriage is not the context within which they want to live their lives. The shoe doesn't fit, so they don't wear it. Few women my grandmother's age had that choice. They shoehorned themselves into the only lives they could imagine and somewhere along the line they started to grumble and complain.

But what did this all have to do with me? I was not my grandmother's twin. Possibilities were open to me that my grandmother could never imagine, because I had other stories to guide me. I could get on the train. I could *drive* the train. And yet I seemed reluctant to do so. I was caught in an odd paralysis. I was freed of the stories that shaped my grandmother, but her own story was still shaping me.

I remember staying with Gran when I was a child. My brother stayed across the hall in Nana and Marj's apartment and slept on their sofa bed, but I had to stay with Gran and sleep in her back bedroom, a small, dark room where the yellowed shades were always pulled. I spent a lot of time in that room. I slept there, but I was also sent there when I was naughty. Gran kept one of her cherished dining-room chairs in that bedroom, and she would set me down on it in the corner. The plastic seat cover that protected the needle-point had gone brittle with age and bit into my legs even through my clothing. The room was dark and—the word comes to me now—murky. It smelled of cracked plastic and of the cigarette smoke that permeated everything in the apartment.

I could never please my grandmother and she often disciplined me, digging into my shoulder with her long red fingernails, shaking me the way a mother cat will shake a kitten. "You always have to have the last word," she'd tell me before she banished me to the bedroom. "You really think you're something. Don't show off. Don't get the big head. Straighten Up. Pipe Down. Be Still."

Be still. This command, more than any other, I remember. I remember her own extraordinary stillness as she sat day after day during her last decades in her light blue, crushed-velvet recliner, perfectly motionless except for the gesture it took to change channels with her remote control or light another cigarette and suck it down. She would exhale smoke from her mouth and then inhale it through her nostrils. "The French do it this way," she told me once.

As an adult, I had fought against her stillness tooth and nail. I was so seldom still that my cats had a preternatural preference for company—they had learned that there was a good chance I would sit down when strangers came and provide a rare lap and a welcoming hand. But I was not accomplishing what I most wanted to achieve, and the reason was more complex than the messages my grandmother passed down to me so directly.

The simple fact was, I feared ending up miserable and alone. I had stories of female success that gave me alternatives inconceivable for my grandmother. But the most powerful of stories, the family stories, did not give me examples of individual success intertwined with love. The stories that had shaped me informed me that I could have personal accomplishment or a happy marriage—I could not have both.

I grew up with three stories for women. The first was, of course, the story of Gran and Marj and Nana, the Three Witches of the West. The problem started with Nana, who was so powerful she chased the priest away and so controlling she wouldn't let her daughters go, and extended through her daughters and their failed marriages. In the story the family told about them, they were managerial women. They put themselves before their partners, they wanted to be in control of their own lives.

The second narrative was my mother's story, a traditional marriage. My mother was happy in her marriage and felt fulfilled as a full-fledged partner in the family enterprise. Still, it was my father's enterprise. Without him, the ranch meant little and she would not have kept it. Her creative accomplishment was the life they had built together. My parents talked openly about death and my mother often expressed the desire to die first. If my father were to precede her, she would have lost the center of her life.

The third story was that of my Great-aunt Marie's marriage to John Bell. I doubt John was an easy man to live with—surely, by today's standards, he was supremely self-centered—but Marie found with him the way to create the life she wanted. The success of their widespread business dealings was due to John, but the ranch was largely Marie's accomplishment. Marie herself, though, took no credit and asserted no visible authority. "I can't remember Marie ever giving me a direct order," a man who worked for her for thirty years once told me. "Even the first day we went out to move cattle, she said, 'How do you think we ought to do this?' I said, 'I don't know, Mrs. Bell. I've never been in this pasture before.'"

As long as I had only these three stories to guide me, I would remain stuck. I didn't have a story that told me I could be visible and not end up alone. But once I understood these stories and the power they held over me, I was free to search out other narratives or write my own. For the first time, I could perceive a relationship fundamentally different from any in my family so far. I could imagine a peer relationship in which I had my work, my partner had his, and we built a home and family together.

Lives don't serve as models, Heilbrun reminded us, only stories do. It was important what I understood of my grandmother's story. If I believed she was miserable and alone because she had a self, I had to believe that I would be miserable and alone because I had one, too. The story told me to destroy myself. But if I believed she was miserable and alone because she had no way to assert her self—in fact, she didn't have any evidence such assertion was possible—then I had to find a way not to diminish myself but to be as large as I was able.

I needed to understand the story of my grandmother's life in order to be free to fully live my own. I had to return to that dark Victorian house, cross the tracks for the first time, and embrace her. Then I could get on the train.

My Life as a Bride

Hal Cannon and me, just married

When I was in college, my mother cut a picture of an evening dress out of a magazine. The dress was floor-length, beautifully gathered around the waist and shoulders, elegant and flowing—a gown for a tall woman. It was not a wedding dress, but she showed it to me and I agreed that it would make for a beautiful bride. And then I laughed and asked her, "Do you have anyone in mind?"

It's the only time I ever remember the two of us talking about a wedding, though we often talked of marriage. That seemed appropriate. We both expected that I would some-day marry, but it was the marriage we focused on, not the event that would launch it. We laughed at *Brides* magazine and the whole bridal culture that suggested that a wedding was a woman's "most glorious day."

And yet. My mother clipped a dress out of a magazine and, secretly, I harbored my own fantasy, romantic and large. It started when I was a small girl. On *my* "most glorious day," I would stand with my true love on the Point, that outlook on top of the breaks from which you can see forever. I imagined a union sanctified not only by ceremony but by the sheer sacredness of space and beauty. The Point was a place for the long view.

By the time I was ready to marry, in the summer of 1991, I was thirty-six years old, my mother had been dead for sixteen years, the ranch had passed out of our family, and I had just moved from Oregon to Salt Lake City to be close to my love, Hal Cannon. When Hal and I began to plan our wedding, I found that I still dreamed of the Point. By then the ranch belonged to an oil company, but I thought the foreman would give us permission.

In May, I took Hal to Cheyenne to meet my father, and then we headed out to the ranch. Wyoming was having an unseasonably wet spring and it was a cold, misty day. By the time we neared Iron Mountain, the fog was so thick we could hardly see a hundred yards in front of us. I gestured off toward the west where the Laramie Range still presumably lay. And on the east, I assured Hal, the breaks started to rise just a mile or so from the road. "It's odd," Hal replied. "I never thought the ranch would look so much like Scotland."

We didn't make it to the Point. We could not have enjoyed the view and besides, the ground was muddy: If we had driven over the prairie on top of the breaks, we would have torn up the ground.

I still thought we would have the ceremony on the Point. Hal could see it in August when we went out for the wedding itself. But August rolled around and the monsoon season continued—the wettest August in anyone's memory. Even the buffalo wallows, those water gaps in Windy Hollow that are *always* caked dry by August, were full.

So it was a trade-off of sorts, the beautiful green hills for the vista from the Point, and that's sort of how the land *is,* in a rural life—generous but persnickety, too, not wanting to give you everything you ask for lest you get the big head or forget who's really in control. But sometimes the land seems to act on its own sort of knowledge. Lovely as the view is from the Point, the Community House, where we had the wedding instead, was a better choice.

Maybe the name, the Community House, says it all. A simple white stucco building built over half a century ago by the local ranchers—Farthings and Hirsigs and Bells and Brownells and McLeases and Jordans and whoever else was around at the time—it is nestled against a hill overlooking Chugwater Creek and the little smattering of now-vacant buildings that once served to locate Iron Mountain on the map. It has a hardwood dance floor, a big stone fireplace with a mantel made from a cottonwood trunk, a bar at one end decorated with all the local cattle brands, lots of windows, and an outhouse in the back. This is where the community gathered for meetings and weddings and school programs, for Halloween and Christmas and New Year's Eve. People would stream in from every direction, laden with food and drink, ready to play.

When I told Biddy Bonham that we wanted to have the wedding at Iron Mountain, she understood better than I what I had in mind. "Of course," she said, "the community will do the food." Biddy was one of my mother's closest friends and she ranches with her husband Wayne, two of their three sons, Bill and Marc, and their daughter Jennie Mai a few miles closer to town, in the ranch area known as Federal.

The "town" of Iron Mountain was never much. At its height, it had a railroad station, a house for a section foreman and a smaller one for the section hand, a school, a cottage for the teacher, a post office, a store, and a few other buildings. The community of Iron Mountain was something altogether larger—two or three hundred square miles that once supported dozens of families. Today, the area supports fewer than ten families and only one, the Farthings, have been there for more than fifteen years. But there is still a sense of community, extending to neighboring areas that have also been depleted, Federal and Horse Creek and even Chugwater, over thirty miles away, and including, too, many people who now live in Cheyenne and Wheatland and Laramie and Rock River but once called Iron Mountain home.

Biddy offered the services of the community because it was the custom of the country. Neither she nor I guessed the extent of her offer. From our original estimate of a hundred, the guest list tripled. If I'd arranged to have the wedding in town, at the Hitching Post or Little America or the Whipple House, where I could organize everything with the catering manager over the phone, the numbers wouldn't have mattered. But an event with a sit-down dinner for three hundred people nearly fifty miles from town in a building without running water, refrigeration, or a stove, when you don't live there and you don't have a mother to just do it for you? It was too much to offer, too much to ask for, too much to accept—in short, the custom of the country.

Over seventy-five people brought food, in an organizational feat more complex and time-consuming than a barn raising. Biddy can witch for water, so attuned to the twitch of a willow rod that she can feel water beneath the surface of the land, and the magic of her touch extends to food. She spiked two hundred pounds of rolled rump roast with garlic and thinly sliced onions, wrapped the pieces in tinfoil and then in burlap, and tied them all with baling wire. Al Schwindt, who had been the butcher at Brannen's Supermarket, the grocery store all the ranchers preferred until the chains put it out of business, cut up the meat and helped Biddy wrap it.

Charlie Farthing mowed several acres of prairie grass around the hall and then he and Bill Bonham dug the barbecue pit. "You tell your father not to worry," he said to me when we inspected it, "this work only cost him three or four cases of beer." The morning before the wedding, at 3 A.M., Charlie and Bill lit the fire in the pit. "Don't let your father worry about that either," Charlie assured me. "We only went through two cases this time." Charlie, Bill, and I were born within two days of each other and we call each other littermates. "You have to understand this relationship," Charlie's wife Carol warned Hal when she first met him. "It's very special and you just have to get used to being a litter-in-law."

Carol offered to make the cake, and when I requested her carrot cake, she bought a hundred pounds of carrots and started peeling. She also organized the dozens of people who brought salad fixings, fruit, and desserts. Glenna Hirsig and her daughter Debby—the Hirsig Ranch once bordered ours and Debby and I attended the one-room school at Iron Mountain together—and Tuda Crews, a friend from Cheyenne, organized the decorations: wreaths made of barbed wire and sagebrush, gilded cowboy boots filled with wild flowers, lariat ropes hung from the rafters with garlands of ribbon. Wayne Bonham took over the sandblasting of the bean pot (it's about the size of a Volkswagen), Jennie Mai built a stone fire ring over which the beans would simmer, and Marc welded a support from which the pot could hang. Half of the ranchers at Horse Creek contributed beans, and one family loaned their motor home for a dressing room, a contemporary touch to an old-fashioned affair and something that will live forever in the local folklore as the "prenuptial R.V."

Perhaps the greatest gift of ceremony is its potential to gather together all the parts of a life. I think of my brother and a cowboy poet friend of Hal's sitting in the Hitching Post Bar the night before the wedding, swapping stories about horses and Harleys and eating the fresh bagels and lox that another friend had just brought in from Seattle. I think of the work party the next day when a friend from New York and another from Montana took a break from their battle with the pack-rat nest in the outhouse to watch eighty-eight-year-old Merrill Farthing walk up to the Community House in the early-morning sun, his arms filled with hundreds of sunflowers. I think about the semicircle of church benches set out on the prairie and the way the thunderheads, which had threatened a cloudburst all afternoon, broke up just before the ceremony and allowed the sun to come through in great golden rays. I think of Hal's brother Roger leading us through our vows, his large eyes liquid with kindness and one tuft of hair standing straight up in the Wyoming breeze. I think of Hal's daughter, Anneliese, standing at his side for the ceremony and my own father giving me away. I think of the coyotes howling the moment the band started to play, and the two babies, Benjamin from the West Coast and Sasha from the East Coast, sleeping side by side in their little bassinets through the hours of music and dancing, just as babies always had in the Community House. I think of watching Bill Bonham and his new friend Dawn Jones, lost in deep conversation. "I bet," Hal remarked, "there'll be another wedding soon." But mostly I think of the mysterious sense of harmony that seemed to wrap around us all, something I can only describe as grace.

"Wouldn't your mother and your Great-aunt Marie have loved this?" Tom Hirsig said to me at one point during the night. "And Sandy," I added, referring to Tom's sister who had been killed in a car accident on the Iron Mountain road. "Yes," Tom said, "Sandy's been here all along."

I realize that anyone who tries to describe her own wedding is suspect, but there *was* something special about the event, something far greater than anything two people could have generated on their own, something that can only exist within community. What was special about our wedding came directly from Iron Mountain, and it had existed years before Hal and I were born.

Iron Mountain is mostly vacant now and yet it is still a community. Its members had come together a few months earlier to commemorate Biddy and Wayne's fortieth anniversary; they will gather again in a few more months to celebrate the marriage of Bill and Dawn. For a hundred years, the community worked because its people had been tied by land and labor and shared destiny. It survives now mostly through habit and memory. If the next couple of decades are as hard on the rural economy as the past ones have been, it will not survive at all.

I left Iron Mountain half by choice and half by necessity. I returned because I needed healing. The community gave me its stories. When I was whole enough for love, it gave me its blessing. I will probably never live in Iron Mountain again, and yet it will always be home, a place I will draw on for strength and which I will fight for, not only in that corner of Wyoming where it actually exists but in the hundreds of other places like it throughout the rural West.

I think sometimes of how different the wedding would have been had we had it on the Point. The pictures would have been stunning, Hal and me silhouetted alone at the edge of the breaks against an endless sky. But perhaps that was just the image my mother and I, so many years before, had wanted to avoid—the wedding, and even the marriage, as something separate from a larger sense of life.

Looking Back

The secret place is gone.
Picked up like a tenant
in the middle of the night
after a bad run of luck,
it trudges down the dark lone road
with the meadow
and the barn
and a long line of cows,
tails bedraggling behind them.
I loved

that secret place
down by the riverbed
hidden by a bank. I whittled
dolls from willows there, made whistles
out of broad-bladed grass, told my big bay
Buddy how I'd never leave.
I lied

though not from will.
Let me be salt
sculpted by cow
tongues until I am lace
and then I am gone.

I want to belong to the ground
again. It is the barn

that breaks my heart
trudging soddenly along, bedsteads
and broken harnesses rocking
softly in the loft, lost
beneath great drifts of
guano. A spavined horse-
collar mirror hangs
cockeyed on the ladder
and that other me looks back
amazed. In the darkness
only one of us is
gone.

NOTES

EPIGRAPH

The quotation is adapted from *Dark and Dashing Horsemen* by
Stan Steiner (San Francisco: Harper & Row, 1981), pp. 169–73.

WALKING THE HOGBACKS: A PROLOGUE

Two other long-time ranches besides the Farthing Ranch are
still in family hands, though the families don't run them. The
children of Jim and Marianne McLeas own the ranch that
belonged to their parents, but they don't live there or run
cattle. The Brownell Ranch has been leased for as long as I
can remember, though Jennine Brownell still lives in the family house.

The Iron Mountain country was homesteaded, which means that what was once federal land was settled. Ranchers in the area today run cattle on private property and negotiate private, state, and railroad leases but do not run on federal ranges.

The list of winds comes from Lyall Watson's delightful book, *Heaven's Breath: A Natural History of the Wind* (New York: William Morrow & Co., 1985), pp. 330–44. Geologist David Love and his wife Jane are two of Wyoming's great treasures and they are immortalized in John McPhee's *Rising from the Plains* (New York: Farrar, Straus & Giroux, 1986). The etymology of "frontier" comes from *The Barnhart Dictionary of Etymology,* ed. Robert K. Barnhart (New York: H. W. Wilson Co., 1988), p. 411. The poet William Pitt Root first brought this etymology to my attention.

Population statistics come from *Statistical Abstract of the United States: 1990* (Washington, D.C.: U. S. Government Printing Office, 1990), p. 637; and *Historical Statistics of the United States, Colonial Times to 1970* (Washington, D.C.: U. S. Government Printing Office, 1975), pp. 467–68.

Mott T. Greene reminded me of our "coming indoors" in *Natural Knowledge in Preclassical Antiquity* (Baltimore: Johns Hopkins University Press, 1992). Forty years earlier, Baker Brownell discussed this in his prophetic but sadly forgotten treatise *The Human Community: Its Philosophy and Practice for a Time of Crisis* (New York: Harper & Brothers, 1950), p. 7:

> The pattern of [humankind's] living, as it were, has been laid out through millions of years in association with living animals and plants and the vast music and movement of the natural world. The form of human life and the structure of its activities are involved in these natural forms and struc-

tures. . . . To abstract human beings by some technological procedure from this functional relationship with the life and creative persistence of the natural world around them would be literally to abstract them from life itself.

Lewis Hyde's book *The Gift: Imagination and the Erotic Life of Property* (New York: Vintage Books, 1979) deals primarily with artists and creativity but has much relevance to community. Hyde discusses what he calls the "genius" of a group on p. 154.

LEGENDS

In these letters of my great-grandfather's, as in other diaries and letters used throughout, I have corrected punctuation for clarity but left spelling and internal capitalizations in their original form.

Wister's letter is in Ben Merchant Vorpahl, *My Dear Wister: The Frederic Remington–Owen Wister Letters* (Palo Alto, Calif.: American West Publishing Co., 1972), p. 18. The altitude on Chugwater Creek is actually closer to 6,200 feet. "How Lin McLean Went East" was published in *Harper's New Monthly Magazine,* December 1892, pp. 135–47.

My grandfather was not the only one to appropriate Wister's westering orphan as a model for his own family history. Judging by the frequency with which these unattached boys—invariably fourteen years of age—turn up in personal memoirs as well as Westerns, one would think that the West was populated by nothing but fourteen-year-old orphans.

Stegner quotes De Voto in *Conversations with Wallace Stegner on Western History and Literature,* Wallace Stegner and Richard W. Etulain (Salt Lake City: University of Utah Press,

1983), p. 149. The de Tocqueville quotation comes from Alexis de Tocqueville, *Democracy in America* (New York: New American Library, 1956), pp. 193–94.

MOTHERS

Louise Bernikow's extended essay, *Among Women,* was published by Harper & Row (New York, 1980). Quotations used here come from pp. 67 and 44. Mary Austin, a contemporary of Jack London, was an important and sadly overlooked voice from the American West. Her *Land of Little Rain* is exquisite. Her mother is quoted in *I, Mary: The Biography of Mary Austin* by Augusta Fink (Tucson: University of Arizona Press, 1983) Dee Brown talks about the "mass maternal force" on p. 284 of *The Gentle Tamers: Women of the Old Wild West* (Lincoln: University of Nebraska Press, 1958). This book was one of the first to try to bring women into more distinct focus. Letters between Owen Wister and his mother are in Fanny Kemble Wister, ed., *Owen Wister Out West: His Journals and Letters* (Chicago: University of Chicago Press, 1958), p. 18. Bernikow quotes Virginia Woolf from "A Sketch of the Past," in *Moments of Being,* ed. Jeanne Schulkind (New York: Harcourt Brace Jovanovich, 1976) on p. 44 of *Among Women.* Bruno Bettelheim talks about the good mother and the bad mother in *The Uses of Enchantment: The Meaning and Importance of Fairy Tales* (New York: Vintage Books, 1989), pp. 66–73.

HOW COYOTE SENT THE WHITE GIRL HOME

Lebedoff actually defined the New Elite on the basis of high IQ, making the point that measures of intelligence, new to this century, combined with opportunity of education to allow and even make inevitable the stratification "by virtue of measured intelligence." The separation, though, comes through higher education. There is plenty of measured intelligence left in the hinterland. I need look no further than my "littermates," Bill Bonham and Charlie Farthing, who still ranch in the Iron Mountain area. When we all took standardized tests in elementary school, they both scored in the high 90th percentiles. But no matter how intelligent Bill and Charlie are, no matter how well read or how well equipped with that older intelligence we call savvy, no matter that Bill has been to college, they are still "Left Behinds" in the eyes of the New Elite (and it is the New Elite who defines such things) because they work with their hands far from the academic world or what critic John Berger calls "the priesthoods of knowledge."

I like Lebedoff's terms and find them useful. Northwestern University philosopher Baker Brownell made a similar observation forty years earlier in *The Human Community:*

It is the persistent assumption of those who are most influential in the modern world that large-scale organization and contemporary urban culture can somehow provide suitable substitutes for the values of the human communities that they destroy. For lack of a better word I call these persons the "educated." They include almost all professionally trained men and women, college professors, upper-bracket educators and businessmen, generals, scientists, bankers, bureaucrats, executives, salesmen, advertising men, big-time publicists, professional artists and promoters, most of the political leaders, and indeed all those most deeply involved by training and by pecuniary and professional interest in the ideology of what is called the modern system. [I would include in this group urban-based environmentalists as well as professionals in agriculture—college-trained managers, bureaucrats in the Department of Agriculture and other agencies, and agricultural engineers, professors, scientists, etc.] . . . These people are by no means all the people in the world, but they are the most influential. . . . Though superficially diversified and often in conflict with each other, they are in many ways a class, definitely at least an elite, or "chosen ones," sitting complacently on their uncriticized assumptions.

. . . They have, indeed, created or helped to create a substitutive culture in which the normal life of men in their communities is being smothered out. It is hardly deliberate, but it is effective. With a fervor based on contempt for little places and the human measure, they advance the trend, as it is called, and promote the ultimate defeat of the human being in the modern world.

An eloquent contemporary voice is Wendell Berry. See *The Unsettling of America: Culture and Agriculture* (New York: Avon Books, 1977) in which Berry discusses, among a great many other things, Jefferson's ideal of education and what happened to it; *Home Economics* (Berkeley, Calif.: North Point Press, 1987); and *What Are People For* (Berkeley, Calif.: North Point Press, 1990). Berry makes the point, as do others, that because we don't see education as a gift, as something which we "take back home," either literally or metaphorically, and because we don't try to reconcile what we learn in the academy with its implications, we have effectively destroyed home community. In his seminal essay "Jefferson, Morrill, and the Upper Crust" in *The Unsettling of America,* Berry traces the way in which higher education and the Land Grant College system have worked to divorce agricultural "professionals" from rural communities and put people out of agriculture.

American Indian Myths and Legends, selected and edited by Richard Erdoes and Alfonso Ortiz (New York: Pantheon Books, 1984), contains many Coyote tales. The quotation comes from p. 335.

NEWTIME: A CALVING DIARY

The order of events in the diary has been changed somewhat for the sake of continuity.

BONES

The epigraph is from the collection of letters *The Delicacy and Strength of Lace,* by Leslie Marmon Silko and James Wright (Saint Paul, Minn.: Graywolf Press, 1985), p. 29.

Yaël Dayan's comments come from her novel, *New Face in the Mirror* (Cleveland, Ohio: World Publishing Co., 1959). A note about the phrase "places in the world a colt can't walk": when a friend read that phrase, she asked if it was a common rural expression. She had just read Janet Kaufman's wonderful collection of short stories about rural midwestern women, *Places in the World a Woman Could Walk* (New York: Alfred A. Knopf, 1983). I had read Kaufman's book some years earlier and had loved it. I was not consciously thinking of it when I wrote that phrase, though Kaufman's language may well have influenced me unconsciously. I'd like to give credit if credit is due.

MARIE

Marie's childhood memory of 2,000 horses is almost certainly exaggerated. According to the livestock inventory for the years 1883–1950 included in Harmon Ross Mothershead's *The Swan Land and Cattle Company, Ltd.* (Norman: University of Oklahoma Press, 1971, pp. 186–88), the largest herd of horses the Swan ever owned was 1,037 in 1883. By the time Marie was a child in the early 1900s, the ranch had around 500. Marie was very young when she saw the great herd, and 500 horses massed in one meadow is impressive enough—something few people living today have ever witnessed.

I had the chance to record several hours of Marie's reminiscences when I worked on my first book, *Cowgirls: Women of the American West* (Garden City, N.Y.: Doubleday, 1982; 2nd ed., Lincoln: University of Nebraska Press, 1992), which includes a chapter on Marie, mostly about her childhood and college years.

THE DEATH OF THE HIRED MAN

The title of this essay comes from Robert Frost's famous poem "The Death of the Hired Man," in *The Poetry of Robert Frost* (New York: Holt, Rinehart & Winston, 1969), pp. 34–40. Employment figures come from *Statistical Abstract of the United States: 1990* (Washington, D.C.: U. S. Government Printing Office, 1990), p. 637; and *Historical Statistics of the United States, Colonial Times to 1970* (Washington, D.C.: U. S. Government Printing Office, 1975), pp. 467–68. In the summer of 1978, I recorded several hours of interviews with Leonard and Lila Cheser.

WRITING MY GRANDMOTHER'S LIFE

Carolyn G. Heilbrun's *Writing a Woman's Life* (New York: Ballantine Books, 1988) is a slim but profound study of the way women have written and talked about their lives—and been written and talked about—and is an indispensable guide for anyone looking at women's material. I have quoted material from pp. 20–25 and p. 37. Heilbrun notes that the letters and diaries of women of achievement often reflected "ambitions and struggles in the public sphere," but when they told their stories in their published autobiographies, "they portray[ed] themselves as intuitive, nurturing, passive, but never —in spite of contrary evidence of their accomplishments— managerial" (p. 24). One study Heilbrun cites that discusses these differences is Jill Conway's "Convention versus Self-Revelation: Five Types of Autobiography by Women of the Progressive Era," Project on Women and Social Change, Smith College, Northampton, Mass., June 13, 1983.

Until recently, even the briefest biographies of Eleanor Roosevelt stressed that she had undertaken her own career for the good of her husband. The quotation used here is from *The Women's Book of World Records and Achievements,* ed. Lois Decker O'Neill (Garden City, N.Y.: Doubleday, 1979), p. 738.

John Briggs talks about the circumstance necessary for prodigy to flourish on pp. 145–46 of *Fire in the Crucible: The Alchemy of Creative Genius* (New York: St. Martin's Press, 1988).

PERMISSIONS
ACKNOWLEDGMENTS